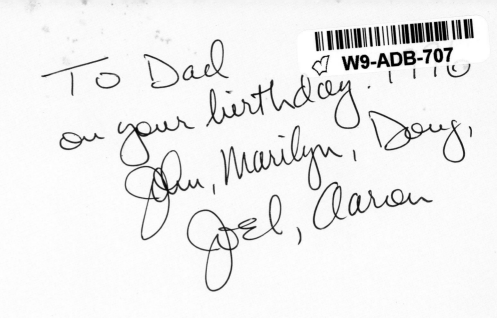

What profit hath man of all his labour
Wherein he laboureth under the sun?

One generation passeth away, and another generation cometh;
And the earth abideth forever.

The sun also ariseth, and the sun goeth down,
And hasteth to his place where he ariseth.

ECCLESIASTES 1:3-5

To Esther.

And to our sons Eric, Bob, and Kurt,
who grew up with this book.
And to Jeanne.
And to my mother and father.

I am thankful for them and the
rest of my family and friends and for
gentle people and beautiful lands.

Prologue

The land and its past

There is serenity now in a place I know like no other. It is around Scales Mound in the deeply etched panorama of Jo Daviess County, in the northwest corner of Illinois, where the land is crayon green in the spring and fleece white in the winter and stays that way until the thaw. Its hills and valleys are sectioned past a thousand horizons with woods and contoured farm fields. There is fish and game. The air smells good. No jet planes scream in the sky, the major highways are two-lane blacktops uncluttered by billboards, and small rivers run under the planks of back-road bridges. The people are kind, go to church, pursue virtue, and work hard with the land. They draw contentment from what they see and hold. Three hundred years ago the discovery of this bountiful land, and lead ore, first lured a migration of adventurers—the French and their "coureurs de bois," then trappers, frontiersmen, miners, speculators, soldiers, fortune hunters—and finally farmers to the untamed wilderness. The Latin word for lead gave nearby Galena its name and made it into a river boom town; even after its decline into peaceful slumber it remained more famous than Jo Daviess County or that place, which seems to me like Biblical Canaan, that I know.

Near here, above the point where Illinois now meets with Wisconsin and Iowa and pierces the carved bluffs of the Mississippi River, Jacques Marquette, an exploring French priest, in 1673 made the first wonderstruck reports on the vistas which lay before his astonished eyes. He noted the existence of lead, the fertility of the

6

land, and the variety of game. It was an invitation to other strong men and soon the sweep westward—and to Illinois country—began. One hundred and seventy-nine years later, John Rudolph Hammer, a farmer from Saxony, Germany, brought his family to a place which rolled into the bottom land of a creek in one of the hidden valleys fifteen miles from Galena. He came to farm. Five generations, echoes of his spirit, came after him. His son, Bernhardt, fathered nine children. Of Bernhardt's children, George Hammer became the father of Willis Hammer. Willis Hammer became the father of Willis Hammer, Jr. Willis Hammer, Jr., became the father of James Alan Hammer, born 110 years after John Rudolph Hammer reached Illinois country. Of the six generations, none rooting far from the old homestead, it is with the lives of Willis Hammer, Jr., his son, his father, and his family, living in the middle years of the twentieth century, that this book is concerned.

I am an Illinois man. Molded by its farms and cities, its people, the shame and pride of its history, I have always delighted in its raw beauty. Perhaps, then, it was fate that led me to the Hammers. For twenty years I have witnessed, in friendship and with a camera, the aging of two generations and the birth of another. They confirmed me to the farm soil. I think that they are unique, but this is not intended as an idolization of their lives. That would shame them. It would be a sin against them. They work hard, love the land, and respect all things in God's world. What is here makes little notice in the swagger of history. Yet the Hammers can hardly be unnoticed. They come from a common mold of the past, that of the uncommon man.

Recently they told me that they had allowed me to make pictures because it was my work and they did not want to deprive me of earning my living. It was a cold winter's day. We were in the kitchen of the home place drinking hot black instant coffee. Bill, Jr., fashioning words for an experience he had never thought would happen, said: "Lot of people like us live and die, but you mean there's going to be a book with our pictures in it, after we're long gone?"

His mother, Mildred, amused at it all, broke in: "Immortalized!"

Bill, Jr., continued: "I don't know what you call it, but a lot of people just live and die and do the same thing we do."

"Maybe so, I said, but there's never been a record of them. Your family is the first."

Now I want to go back to the very beginning because this is where I think the Hammer story starts. In the creation, in what was destined to become Illinois, there were great convulsions before the earth settled and shallow seas were formed. In cycles of millions of years the seas retreated, then came again to submerge the land. With each submergence strata of sediment were deposited. In one period lead-bearing dolomite was laid down in the Galena area, and—indeed, as in Genesis—the waters were finally gathered away and dry land appeared. Erosion carved the land, creased it and made it rugged with valleys and ridges. Then great ice drifts came and scraped away nine-tenths of the ruggedness from the Illinois landscape. But these glaciers slipped past Jo Daviess County, leaving untouched this terrain, which looks today much as the whole of the state probably did before the Ice Age.

After the ice drifts, the stage was set for mankind. Asians first, fifty thousand years before the empires of Europe established lacy fringes of culture on Eastern shores. For the French, exploration gained them Indian friendships and vast lands which they dotted with pleasant settlements and beautiful-sounding names. In the upper Mississippi lead country, in 1721, they searched for silver, bringing with them seven hundred miners, of whom five hundred were Dominican slaves. But they found only lead and, disappointed, most of them left. They had used a map published in Paris in 1703, charting "La Rivière de la Mine." This river, which spurs into the

Mississippi, eventually became known as the Le Fevre River—then the Fever River. Today it is the Galena River. For the next hundred years, only some crude lead mining went on.

Then came a period of chaos ending with colonial revolution and conquest. The French had Indian alliances, the British had troops, ports, and supplies, but the colonials were resolute. Out of this struggle and a new push westward, the American was formed. Shaped by it, he now shaped the land. The map of Illinois was changed four times. Finally, in 1818, it became a state, but not before its northern boundary had been argued fifty-one miles to its present border to include a shoreline, Chicago, and the driftless barrens of Jo Daviess County.

Settlers now came to Illinois, and from them grew the legendary character of the American and the Midwestern farmer of even later migrations. They came from the coastal states, the Ohio and Cumberland river valleys, Tennessee, and Kentucky with wagons or flatboats loaded with tools, rifles, animals, and furniture. Back East, men wore silver and lace. The settlers wore deerskin and homespun and lived in log cabins. Some knew the Bible; a few could read it. They were mostly poor, decent farmers, fishermen, and frontiersmen. To them to be good was to be manly: independent, potent, rugged, silent and wary, never betraying. Their women believed this and so did their children. They had already conquered a wilderness with their long rifles, axes, faith, hard work, and cocky courage. They were going to do it again. Yet these were an uncommon people of dreams, who, though they loved the virgin lands, could blink their eyes and see tilled fields, nice houses, stock grazing, and a good water supply.

The settlers fanned out across the state toward the Mississippi, but few went to the Fever River until 1823, when the first steamboat entered it and the first licensed smelter ended the era of crude lead mining. A drift of migration toward the mines began, and a boom came with the opening of the Erie Canal in 1825. Swarms of migrants came to Illinois. A year later Galena was laid out and miners looking for diggings discovered the upper east fork of the Fever River, in the vicinity of what would become Scales Mound. At this time Conrad Lichtenberger, a veteran of the War of 1812, came from Pennsylvania, built a cabin, and cleared ten acres of land with an ax and a grub hoe. He was the first to raise a field of corn, his was the first white child to be born there, and his too—another daughter, at age seventeen—was the first to die.

Jo Daviess County was organized in 1827. In the following two years lead diggings made it the scene of the country's first big mining rush. Galena was turned overnight into a city of thirty thousand canvas-and-bark tents. There were Yankees, Hoosiers, Buckeyes, Corn Crackers, Pukes, Badgers, and Suckers. "There is no civil law here," complained one Massachusetts man. "Neither law nor Gospel can pass the rapids of the Mississippi." Some of these men abandoned mining, staked claims to government lands, and began farming. John Sole, in 1830, sold his cabin and claim at the base of a mound to a man named Samuel H. Scales. Scales built a public house there, along the stagecoach line, and the mound took his name. The town of Scales Mound grew up about a mile away.

By 1832 a semblance of order came to Jo Daviess County, marred only briefly by Black Hawk, the war chief of the Sauk and Fox Indians. The Indians had the land; in a devious act the government bought it, and miners, first heading for Galena, saw its fertility and claimed it. Where Indians once hunted, buried their dead, and grew corn, settlers' cabins and fields now stood. Black Hawk, outraged, began raiding. A volunteer army, which included Abraham Lincoln, was mustered. Farming and mining operations were suspended, and the settlers of Scales Mound gathered in a nearby fort atop Charles Mound, the highest point in Illinois. The wars ended at the Battle of Bad Ax, where the army massacred

SCALES MOUND,
FOR WHICH THE TOWN
WAS NAMED

Black Hawk's people. The next year the tribes of the state ceded all their lands and moved west. The Indian was gone from Illinois.

More land was now available to satisfy the growing demand. By 1836 the railroad had surveyed the land around Scales Mound. It took about a dozen days to travel from Chicago by wagon, ten days from St. Louis to Galena by river steamboat. Scales Mound, only ten miles away from Galena on the stage line, was on the edge of the frontier, but Galena was the rich metropolis of the Northwest. It was publishing a newspaper, building a library, churches, schools, and elegant mansions in styles reflecting the architectural experience of the whole country. Then, suddenly, the prosperous days of Galena were over. The surface veins of lead were exhausted, the gold rush of '49 lured people away, and the river began to silt in, making the channel unnavigable for cargo boats. Jo Daviess County settled into farming.

With Europe still shaken by the Napoleonic Wars, migration to

THE MODERN HIGHWAY FOLLOWS THE OLD STAGECOACH LINE

CONRAD LICHTENBERGER'S GRAVE IN THE SCALES MOUND CEMETERY

America continued. Guidebooks told the immigrant of Illinois rivers, of land where corn had grown on inexhaustible soil for a hundred years, of game and abundant wild fruit of all kinds, of farmers with several hundred hogs, two hundred cattle, twenty horses, a thousand sheep. English, Irish, and German families slowly came to the county and settlements became towns.

At this time in Germany the farmers wanted to be free of their remaining feudal obligations. In America they could find freedom and unlimited land. A man could prosper by working hard. John Rudolph Hammer took his family from the German countryside and migrated to America. They went west over historic trails, the pioneer past entering into them as they entered Illinois country. When they reached Scales Mound in 1852 and bought some land from the railroad, only a little of the edge of the wilderness had been dulled. The source of the Mississippi had not yet been discovered. The population of the state was 851,490. The railroad owned two million acres and was selling it for from five to twenty dollars an acre. In one year Scales Mound would be a town, in three the railroad would arrive, and in eight the Civil War would begin.

Like others before him, Hammer began to subdue the land with ax and plow. He built a house and with three other men founded a church. His family multiplied and he saw that what he had done was good.

Now, to the east of the Mississippi, on the old Chicago-Galena stagecoach line to Scales Mound and then a little beyond John Rudolph Hammer's homestead, the Willis Hammer home place lies in the seclusion of a hollow. You cannot find the farm except by luck; you have to be shown. On land laced by roller-coaster gravel roads, you go up ridges, down into valleys, and along river bottoms. Cattle and horses graze, hawks circle, jackrabbits dart into the road. In the woods, although you cannot see them, are deer.

The winters are hard, long and cold; the growing season is less

than five months. Snow lingers until the thaw and rain wet the earth. Soon the land is covered with the mist of soft green grasses coming alive. The countryside is transformed into splashes of color. Next comes spring planting, and though it may have been late, by summer the contoured fields are ringed with the furrows of emerging crops. In July, with hot days and dry fields, mature hay is cut but corn crops are in danger of drought. Somehow, the rains always come to bless the soil, and the corn grows so fast you can hear it. You can also hear a calf call out and a cow bellow back. So many birds sing that you feel each of your movements is orchestrated, and when you walk, instead of the monotonous thud of shoes on city pavements, you hear the sounds of earth, twigs, stones, and grass. When autumn comes, barns and silos are full of the harvest of spring and summer work. Now the flayed soil and the forests with their orange and yellow leaves luminous against a blue sky go to rest. Then it is winter again. The air is frigid. At a distance, red barns are like linoleum patches on a background of brilliant snow, and you can see puffs of breath coming from a farmer doing his chores, tending his land and feeding the stock committed to his care. All is crisp and pure.

On such a winter day in 1954, over a hundred years after John Rudolph Hammer homesteaded there, his great-great-grandson, Billy Hammer, aged thirteen, waited to meet me on his back road, which butted into the blacktop that covered the old stage line. He smiled an easy greeting. His sister had won a Singer sewing contest and I had come to make her picture for a magazine. As Billy led me into the generations of his family's land, I felt I was entering a storybook scene—Brigadoon, Camelot, and the Biblical Canaan all at once. I met his family and felt an immediate comfort with them. I made my pictures, ate delicious food, and witnessed their joyful appreciation of their way of life and the loving kindness they showed each other.

Later, I kept remembering the time I had spent with the Hammers, and when summer came I went back to visit. To my surprise, Billy had grown almost a whole head taller and his joy of life had increased proportionately. I made a picture of him walking alongside his father, who was driving the tractor. That struck off an idea: one day I would make a picture of Billy and *his* son—of course there had to be a son—in the same way. And so began this project, with no end in mind except to preserve the happy days of my visits to the farm and the true life story of a boy growing to manhood, a boy who admires his father and his ways and wants them for himself.

In that same year, 1954, a marine sergeant on the drill fields of Quantico barked: "Are your rifles clean? They better be, because Dien Bien Phu just fell." Off the coast of Vietnam, a contingent of leathernecks was waiting to land. In the years which followed I photographed Billy Hammer growing up on the farm while other young farmers were compelled to leave it for the city; Americans faced student revolts, drugs, pollution, population explosion, and the warning of a university professor that the 1970s would see a disastrous world famine. Looking for where they belonged, young people moved into communes, long hair became fashionable, families split over issues, Beatle music rocked tradition, health-food stores opened everywhere, Jesus freaks proclaimed themselves, and government scandal produced a new dictionary meaning to an old word: Watergate. Pornography in neighborhood movie theaters prospered while *The Saturday Evening Post, Collier's, Look,* and *Life* went under. Trains gave way to giant jets and people hopped around the world on cheap excursion fares, hardly ever discouraged by skyjackers. The Middle East was torn by war, the Berlin Wall stood, tanks rolled against Freedom Fighters, foreign alliances shifted, and protests were more audible than ever. The price of everything went up. And John F. Kennedy, Robert F. Kennedy, and Martin Luther King were shot dead.

I had traveled a great deal, here and abroad, but came back to Jo Daviess County periodically to make pictures. After one of my closest friends was killed photographing a war I went out to the farm to reassure myself that the world, somewhere, still made sense.

In the morning the sun rises over the ridge and you truly know the day has begun. Roosters really crow, cows moo, pigs "oink," church bells toll, and streams swish and gurgle. People work, pray, and play. They sew doilies, quilt, can food, bake wonderful cakes, and eat well. The ground smells the way ground should, the tractor groans power, the manure spreader enriches the earth, the bees fly to clover, a neighbor on a dusty road waves as he passes in a pickup, the hay is sweet, the scent of silage is slightly intoxicating, the farm dog runs barking alongside the sheep or cattle he herds, the crickets sing, the birds go about their business. Everything goes about its business in a natural way. In the evening the sun goes down over another ridge, and you know you have lived a sensible day.

These were the images I was thinking about when I drove out to the Hammers after it had been decided that my pictures and notes were to be put into book form. I had taken the road to the Hammer farm many times over the years. Places along it had become landmarks to thoughts I had had when I went by them for the first time. Now they prompted a review—the philosopher was right when he said: "Life is lived forward and understood backward."

I carried with me a tape recorder and a case full of pictures of the years I had photographed the Hammers and their land. There had never been much talk among us—it was as though I had been involved in a motion picture without a sound track—and there are things that can be understood only through words. So with the pictures in front of us, the tape recorder turned on, we reviewed the past. As we looked at the pictures we remembered, talked about, and understood what had taken place. The sound track had been added.

20

Farm Boy

Archie Lieberman
FARM BOY

Harry N. Abrams, Inc., Publishers · New York

Library of Congress Cataloging in Publication Data
Lieberman, Archie.   Farm boy.
  1. Farm life—Pictorial works.   I. Title.
S521.L467   917.73'03'4   73-12231
ISBN 0-8109-0148-X

Library of Congress Catalogue Card Number: 73-12231
© Copyright 1974 in the United States by Archie Lieberman

Printed and bound in the United States of America

Contents

What it means to love the land

For over half a century Willis Hammer, Sr., has been working hard on the land, milking cows twice a day, doing the never-ending chores, fighting the extremes of nature and market prices in the valley in which he was born and which he has never left. The eyes and hearts of three generations of Hammer men before him knew this land, too. Now his children and grandchildren are heirs to all that. A quiet man, he is sparing with words.

BILL, SR.   We used to milk twenty, twenty-five cows in the early days. Now we're milking seventy to eighty. I still enjoy it all. I really do. I'd sooner milk than anything. Why?

Mildred Evans Hammer grew up on a farm near Shullsburg and has been his wife since he brought her to the valley over thirty-five years ago. She has worked hard alongside him in yard, house, field, and in raising their two children. She understands what he means to say.

MILDRED   Why? Because you love farming, because you love someone. Before we got machines, I helped him milk by hand out there in the yard. I'd shove one cow out of the way and sit down to another one. In summertime, we wouldn't even put them in the barn, we'd put them in the yard. It would be, "Bill, did you milk this one?" "Yep," and I'd shove her out of the way. "Did you milk that one?" You know, Bill's been here for close to sixty years. When we were first married, we were eight years over to the Hesselbachers' working there. We've been only here and over the field to there and back. Sure, there's been lots of hard work. But you either love farming or get out of it.

BILL, SR. I heard someone once say that Americans love the land like they love their own skin, and they love work in the same way. I think that's one of the things of being a farmer. Enjoying farming. You love the land—to plant things and see it grow, and you enjoy the hard work that goes with it. That's farming. I think any farmer loves the land. I don't think you'd ever make a good farmer unless you really enjoyed doing it or working with it. I don't think I'd care to do anything else.

MILDRED After you get to raising your own chickens, potatoes, and things, you don't care for bought ones. When you have a little garden of your own, you think more of that than something you buy. It's your own from the start. The same as your child is your own from the start. It's a seedling and it grows with you. The land is like a child. Yes. And you grow with it. It's like a revolving thing. As a child, you grow up with the land and it takes care of you, and then one day you plant and it grows as a child does, and you take care of it.

Like his mother and father, Bill, Jr., has worked with the land in the same place all his life. He has also worked very hard. His father's farm was not large enough to support two families after Bill, Jr., married Dorothy Hickman from nearby Scales Mound, and he had to strike out on his own. By working on shares, taking extra jobs outside the farm, sometimes working two days without sleep, he was able to buy a farm and go into partnership with his father. He had always wanted to continue the life of his father, grandfather, great-grandfather, and great-great-grandfather before him. Today most young people in rural areas must go elsewhere to find their opportunities. Bill, Jr., is lucky. He can farm. He sees no other way but farming for himself.

30

Out here it's always changing; it's always different or doing something different. No day is exactly the same. It's a challenge and it's a recycling. Each spring you start plowing, planting, then it grows, you harvest—it's just a constant recycle. The land for me is a way of living, of being free and independent. You get to use your own brain and you're not just working for a paycheck.

What I really like about it is when you're alone, like when you spray corn. You're by yourself and you're just constantly looking at a beautiful picture. It isn't the same every day. The trees are blowing different, there's fresh air and the different seasons. I can spend sixteen hours by myself and not talk to anybody. You think about what your troubles are, if some trouble is going on, that you got to try and solve. Sometimes you do a little dreaming about what you can do or where you're going, about your family and having a nice place, to have it paid for and own it all yourself. And to keep it.

I've got my place now, I've got it and I don't want to let go of it, no part of the land. It's just like this old rock house I have. A guy comes down and tells me I could get a lot of money for it. I'm just not interested. I would sooner have things the way they are than have the money and let go of them. I like the way things look around here, and I like to keep people at a distance. I mean, I like being alone. I wouldn't like being completely alone. I like my family around. That's enough. I don't need any more. We have lots of friends that come visiting on holidays, or things, and that's nice, too.

Then, out here, it's a matter of putting the crop in and getting it to grow big. That means a lot of work. But a farmer is someone who likes to work and enjoys seeing stuff grow. That keeps him on the land. Sometimes you get a little tired. Then you change to a different crop, a different job, and it's like starting in new again. Like baling hay : at first it's new, then it gets old, but then you'll be switching to another way—chopping it or something—and it starts in all new again. And the time goes fast; sometimes you don't even know what day of the week it is, and you're always surprised that one season is over and another is here.

The seasons and the weather—that's the main topic of discussion around here. Sometimes it's too dry, too wet, too cold, or too hot. You get irritable, but you just figure it's the way it's supposed to be, I guess. You just got to take what the Lord'll give you, and that's about it. If He thinks it's enough rain when you think you need more, then I guess it's going to be enough rain. You have to accept that—no need fighting it, no sense in growling about it. Like last year it was too wet. Now it's too dry. But for as wet as it was last year—we didn't think we'd get anything—we had as good a corn crop as we ever did.

Farmers do a lot of grumbling, that's true. You get a little worried or frustrated when you don't think you're going to get a crop, or on those days when everything is working against you. But you have to work the land because it's what you got. You can't really get mad at it and expect something from it. It wouldn't do much good to cuss it. People can talk back to you and tell you what they want. The only way the land will tell you it won't get a good crop is that you won't get a very good crop. So, you got to be alert to catch it before you have a bad crop. The land only does what you do to it. If you don't take care of it, it won't take care of you. You got to like it. Just like the animals. If you want to go out and beat your cows and be cruel to them, they won't give very much milk. You got to like them and pamper them. In order to get milk out of a cow, you can't beat it. The same way as the land. You got to love it all. Like a day that we might like for ourselves isn't the proper day for growing corn. A good miserable humidity day, hot, where you can hardly stand it, is a perfect day for growing corn. That's nature, and it's sort of a partner in all you do. It teaches you and you learn something every year. Mostly you learn to live with it. Everything will turn out all right

32

anyhow. If the Lord wants it that way, I guess that's the way it's going to have to be.

DOROTHY   When you talk about land, to me the farm is the land. I love the farm because it's someplace that's just ours. Working it makes you like it more when you know it's your own. But I don't stop and think about it all the time. The land is here; it's what we make our living off. When I work on it, doing some of the men's work, well, it's just something that has to be done. Bill likes to climb up a hill in the summer and sometimes I go with him. You look down and see those fields you've planted and worried over, and they're growing good. You feel good. It's beautiful, the gold of the oats and the green of the corn.

BILL, SR.   When you see things growing, growing up out of seeds, you know all you could do was plant them and take care of them. It's impossible for a human to make seeds without the help of Him. You make a tractor out of a lot of artificial stuff, but you can't make all the different kinds of plant seeds.

MILDRED   One of the best explanations I ever heard was at Sunday school. Once, when a child said he didn't know if there was a God or not, the teacher got kind of provoked and she said, "You mean to tell me that you can put a little black seed in the ground and you'll get a red plant with a white center and a green top, which is a radish, and you don't believe in God? Nothing else could do it!" There's a lot of them that don't go to church and they might say they don't believe in God. What is it they don't believe in then?

Cletus Hammer, a cousin, sat on his porch railing during one of those languid summer days just before evening milking. From his house, on top of a hillside where fieldstone had been placed in an embankment by his grandfather,

33

Bernhardt, he could see far. Below him was Mill Creek. Across that, away in the distance, Bill, Jr., could be made out cutting hay. Cletus's wife, Wilma, had just gotten into the pickup to bring the cows out of the pasture to the barn.

CLETUS   This was all railroad land in 1849. This was when all this started. When railroads first went through the country, they took a strip of land fifteen or twenty miles on each side of the track. Eventually they decided to sell some of that and then, like homesteading, you could purchase it from them. Right down over there, along the creek, my great-grandfather Rudolph went and settled. He was the first owner of the land to do anything with it after the railroad let loose of the land.

When I was a little kid, I used to think that my grandfather was a harsh man. But he had his reasons. My dad and grandfather lived up to the old Bible where it says the man is the head of the household. Hammers have a trait of being more or less content. My dad never traveled far and I don't have to. We have so many kinds of recreation right on our own farm. We have a nice stream for fishing, we have hunting. I can hunt deer, squirrels, rabbits—anything you want to hunt. I got them here, right on the farm. I don't have to travel.

Wilma returned after getting in the cows. She said: "Cletus has never been anyplace else. This is where he has always been. His roots are really planted here."

CLETUS   That's true. But I think I love this land, all right. I have a different feeling of what it means to love the land than what someone else might have. To me the land is my being. It's all I've got. It's my existence. People come out from the city and they say, "Beautiful," but all they see is the top beauty, what they can see with the eye. I don't even see that. I feel like I'm just a part of it; and when you read

36

in the Bible where it says God gave you this land to till it, to take care of it, to prosper, that's what it means to me. That is my duty to do this. I don't consider it a job exactly. It's a duty. A responsibility. That gives me my happiness and satisfaction and a reason for being here.

The joys of growing up on the farm-1955

Under the ever-changing skies which form the heavens over his place, Willis Hammer, Jr., grew up. By the time he was fourteen he was known as Junior, Butch, Billy, and Bill. Work has always been a joy to him, because he was outside and with his father. Unhappiness is not natural to him. He has always had chores. At three he fed the dog and followed his father around; at six he got the cows out of the pasture; at nine he milked, even though he was still not strong enough to lift the fifty-pound milk bucket; at ten—though his mother worried about the hills—he was driving the tractor; by the time he was twelve, he could do a man's work; and at thirteen he made a motor scooter, using wheelbarrow wheels and a chain-saw engine, and rode it to chase cattle when he wasn't rounding them up on a horse.

Until the seventh grade, he walked a mile to a one-room country schoolhouse, where there were eight students. That was abandoned the next year for a consolidated school in Scales Mound. Billy didn't like school. It took him away from the real world on the farm. He joined the Boy Scouts but attended only three meetings. "That was for kids who don't have anything to do." He preferred chasing sheep with his dog alongside him, resting in the barnyard under a tree that must have sheltered his grandfathers, rounding up a newborn calf on horseback, doing a man's work with the haying, riding wildly through the land at sunset, strutting freely in the old oak tree, walking through a field under a summer sky.

It was something to see, the way Billy followed his father around. A neighbor recalled those early times: "When Butch was little, about three he started, he was allowed to take a horse and follow his dad all the time. Always with his dad on an old horse. He had a black horse, I can't think what the name

of it was. He went everywhere on that horse. He just followed his dad just to be with him. He learned a lot. No matter what Old Bill would be doing, Butch'd know what was going on. There was interest there."

Willis Hammer, Sr., had three brothers and a lot of work to do. That was a joy to him. He works the same land that he did when he was a child.

BILL, SR. We boys were always fighting around. My mother couldn't see this as fun. She'd get angry and start talking in German. I never knew what it meant, but it seemed like it was her favorite expression and then she'd always say, "Here, you boys, stop it, stop it!" I couldn't tell what the German meant, but I knew you better be on your best behavior.

Out here you don't have nobody but the people around you. People who live on a farm have a lot to do with their brothers. In those days we did all the farming with horses. We broke horses for other people—riding and driving horses, Percherons and Morgans. There was an excitement and challenge to break horses. There were a lot of good things. That's a long time ago, hard to remember all the things, except that there was a good feeling. There's no better life than a farm life for a family being close together. You work together, you're close together. It was good when my mother made ice cream. In those days you didn't go and buy ice cream like you do now. With all her other work, you knew she cared for you when she worked on making ice cream. When the folks'd go to Galena, they'd usually bring back some corn flakes. That was special. It was a Sunday morning dish. We liked things like that and the work.

I started young doing chores. I was about ten when I started plowing with the horses and milking cows. We have a good life here. We've never had a complete crop failure, but sometimes we have some pretty bad weeks—animals die; in the winter the cold creeps into your bones—these are not the joyous weeks. But as soon as the grass gets green and the days get warmer and longer, everything is good again.

Bill, Jr., liked the stride of his father and tried to fit into his footprints.

BILL, JR.   I liked being around him. It was fun learning to do things I saw him do, to respect him and what he was doing, and I'd want to learn the job, too. Then the day came when he'd let me do something. Then in a year I'd be a little older and he'd start me in on something new. It was a joy learning and thinking that you're a man before you really are. If I was figuring that I was throwing bales on like a man, I'd throw twice as hard. There are things about farm life that might seem like work, but they're fun. We used to burn wood, so I had to put wood in the wood box.

If I wasn't busy with chores, I could find other things to do. I'd go out in the barnyard and bulldog calves, or try to ride them like they do in the rodeo. You'd get a pretty good-size calf and get on it and see how long you could ride before it could throw you off. Sometimes we'd get company, and they'd bring kids and we'd have plenty of space to run around.

Some things I'd do over differently. I'd have liked to have been smarter when I moved out of the country school and went to town. The kids there gave me a pretty rough time because I was a farm kid. City kids and farm kids are altogether different. If I had known a little more before I went to town, they wouldn't have given me such a rough time. Scales Mound might not be considered a big town, but at that time it was the main town around here. On Saturday nights you couldn't walk around the aisles in the stores—there was that many people in there. I looked forward to going there. A bunch of us country kids would go in there and buy a watermelon and fill up on it. And we used to have fights with the town kids. We were country kids going into town, and they didn't particularly like it.

Most of the time I spent alone. When I was younger, before I got to riding horses regular with farm neighbor kids, I was mostly alone except for Saturdays and Sundays, when we might have company. I

54

had friends, other kids around the country. But Dad was my best friend.

MILDRED   He was born at my sister's, April 8, 1941. We didn't go to the hospital in those days, you know. That was no serious thing, having a baby, and I went to my sister's and she took care of me. We had a doctor come and I was scared to death of the doctor. He was an old grouch.

Bill was working the morning the doctor was coming to get the baby's name. We had said we were going to name him John. I was lying there in bed and going, "John Hammer, John Hammer—oh heavens, someday they'll call him Jack Hammer. I can't stand that!" So the doctor came and he asked me if I had a name picked and I said we were going to call him John, but I don't like Jack Hammer, and that's what he'd get called. And I said, "I think I'll call him Junior. His dad don't know it, but I think I'm going to call him Junior." The doctor said he'd put that down but to call him if we had to change it. I thought, "That's better than telling him I haven't got a name picked and have him pick my head and tell me, 'You had nine months to pick a name, why don't you have one?' Bill came that night and I said, "I gave the doctor his name today. You know what I called him?"

He said, "What?"

I said, "Well, it's Hammer, Jr."

I looked at him and he looked at me and he said, "Couldn't you think of a better name than that?"

And I said, "Nope!"

I was real happy that I gave him a son and named him after Bill.

I wanted Junior to grow up in his footsteps—and he did.

BILL, JR., BEING MEASURED ON THE BARN BY HIS PROUD MOM—A FAMILY RITUAL OF MANY YEARS

September, 1959

It was four years since Mildred had painted the mark on the door. Now, Bill, Jr., was eighteen. He was through with school and was working full time with his father. The truck door now read "Willis A. Hammer & Son." It was a proud moment for both of them when that addition went on. The farm needed some new things, and Mildred went off to work to help get the cash. But before leaving each morning she would make sure her men had enough food for noontime dinner. The men, as before, spent a lot of time with each other and enjoyed it. Around them the family was growing. Janet had married Bill Brickner, and they had two little girls. Bill Brickner had grown up in Scales

DOROTHY AND BILL, JR.,

Mound. He was a good enough ball player to be considered for the major leagues, but he gave that up and bought a farm adjoining the Hammers', working both there and at a job in a nearby city. Sometimes he would work with Bill, Sr., and Billy, cutting trees on one of the wooded hillsides on their property.

Billy liked to think that four years before he "didn't even have a driver's license and was far from thinking about having a girl." Now he had both. He started going with Dorothy Hickman. Dorothy lived on a farm a mile out of Scales Mound. The old stagecoach road went by it. There, with her father and mother, Kenneth and Celia, and with her brother and sister, Bob and Phyllis, she grew up. Billy never really considered her a farm girl; she lived too close to town, even though her father was a general farmer and her mother worked hard as a farm wife.

BILL, SR.

MILDRED

JANET AND BILL BRICKNER WITH THEIR DAUGHTERS, BONNY AND BRENDA

DOROTHY'S PARENTS, KENNETH AND CELIA HICKMAN, HER SISTER, PHYLLIS, AND HER BROTHER, BOB

DOROTHY   One of the best things was to go after the cows and their calves. There were all these little paths that the cows would make, and we'd have fun trailing those things around, taking a new one each time and watching the way the cows would all follow. I liked the farm up there. It was pretty. In the summer we went walking out in the pastures. It was nice, especially in late afternoon when things would start to cool off. I always enjoyed that, walking around out there. I liked that particular place. It was home.

That is where Billy courted her. They would walk out in the field on a summer evening, and her brother Bob would tag along with the old collie.

Bill, Sr., felt good about Bill's growing to manhood, having him work with him, and seeing him go with Dorothy.

BILL, SR.   I thought it was pretty nice. He was growing in a direction I thought was good. But he always had his own choice of whether he wanted to be a farmer or do something else. I tried to make it interesting enough by keeping up with the newer ways of doing things so that maybe he would stay on and be a farmer. Underneath it was a kind of way of hoping that he sure would follow in my footsteps.

MILDRED   Butch and I dispute about when he started going with Dorothy. He had her picture in his billfold and I found it when they were just kids. He tells me today he didn't, but he did. From the time he started town school, up there, he knew her. But, then, they never went steady. They'd go for a while and then they'd decide they were tired of each other and they would go try greener fields.

BILL, JR.   When I first knew Dorothy, or remember knowing her, was when I went to town to grade school. I was in the eighth grade and she was in sixth. Just thought she was a younger grader, didn't even think she was a girl. But then when I was a freshman she was in eighth grade

64

and I dated her, but that was just one date. We didn't hit it off too good. It was my first date. We had to go with a friend of my sister's because they were an older couple. We went to a dance up at school. It was a couple of years before I took her out again.

Then, when I was a senior, we started going together and then we broke up for about nine or ten months. We always had arguments, but we liked each other. I guess she wanted to do more things than I was used to doing. She ran around with a couple of girls who lived in town, and she lived close by. They were up town more than I ever was. I didn't ever know for sure if, when I got married, I'd marry a farm girl, but I figured she'd have more in common with me. I started in going with another girl. I still liked Dorothy, but I wasn't about to let her know it for a while. I probably, more or less, took up with this other girl to make Dorothy jealous. I always found that if you chased them they wouldn't have anything to do with you. She got jealous and came after me one night.

DOROTHY   The first recollection I have of Bill was at a church roller-skating party. I must've suddenly noticed boys. I was about fourteen. I wasn't interested in boys before that. But that was where I got to know him. Be around him. I knew his sister Janet through 4-H. She was a cheerleader and interested in the same things I was. I used to think, "She is really great." She went out with Brickner, and all that. They were really quite a couple, but at that time I never thought about her little brother.

I always liked his smile. He always had a cute smile. Still does. I knew that some day I was going to marry him before he knew that. When I was a junior, I was queen of our prom. He was going with a girlfriend of mine. I went with another boy. I remember that when I saw him with this girl I just knew that shouldn't be. We'd been going together and then we broke up. We fought a lot. He didn't like me talking to other people but I liked to. He was really jealous. So was I.

I flirted around, I was younger then. I got a friend to tell Bill I wanted him to dance with me. He wouldn't. He was still angry with me. After the prom I went to a girlfriend's house and stayed all night. All we talked about was Bill. I finally woke to the fact that he was the one I wanted to go with. But he started going steady with this other girl. It was May sixth. I was in town. So was he, and when I saw him drive out of town I followed him. He went past our place, and I kept on right behind him. He knew something was up. He turned off the blacktop onto his side road. Finally he stopped on down by Brickners' gate. We got out and talked and then we started going together.

I never thought when I was growing up that I wanted to be a farm wife. I just wanted to be a wife and mother. My mother worked hard, right along with my dad. Milked cows every night and every morning. I thought that was a hard life. I knew that Bill wanted to be a farmer when he was courting me and that I'd be a farmer's wife. It didn't seem bad. I wasn't thinking about that. I was just thinking about being with him.

BILL, SR., BILL, JR., AND BRICKNER FELL AN OAK TREE

The twenty-fifth anniversary-1959

They had worked side by side to build the farm up, and had a daughter and a son to whom they taught their own ways, which were honorable and according to the Good Book. They also had grandchildren, their daughter's girls. All the family still lived in the valley. They had love for each other and the respect of their neighbors. These twenty-five years of marriage, good and bad, belonged only to Bill and Mildred and were their profit and their happiness.

To celebrate their anniversary, the Hammers held a reception in Scales Mound at the Flamingo Tea Room, a place built in 1910 as an implement shop. Friends, neighbors, and relatives came with presents and good wishes, and their parked cars jammed South Railroad Avenue. The talk hummed of the weather, the crops, and memories. It was a day of warm contentment, and at the end of it the sun made the skies a cycloramic curtain.

Even on this day, however, there were the chores. Having taken the work from his father, Bill, Jr., paused for a moment in the doorway of the milking barn. He looked out on the dimming autumn mist rising from the ground and thought about what was next for him.

BILL, SR. I was doing chores for my brother, and in between chores I went to town. I met a friend. He didn't have a car and I did; it was a 1930 or '33 Durant. He wanted to know if I wanted to go on a double date that night. I said, "Sure." Mildred was his date. I was taken with her. I don't know if it was that night or at a dance afterwards when I asked her for a date.

BILL, SR., AND MILDRED CHAT AT THE GATE BEFORE THE EVENING MILKING

JANET, MILDRED, BILL, SR., AND BILL, JR.

MILDRED   Bill was about eighteen. I was sixteen.   He was with another boy in Scales Mound. It was Sunday afternoon, and maybe they were playing pool. This boy had a date with me that night, but he didn't have a car. This boy wanted Bill, who had a car, to bring him to see me. They called up and wanted to know if I could get a date for Bill. I got a girl for Bill and I went with my date, and we went to a show in Shullsburg. It was in the winter time, and a real snowy night. Bill was driving, and we took his date home first, because she lived closer to town than I did. Then, going to my home, we had to go up a big, steep hill called White's Hill, and we couldn't make it up. Bill had to get out and put chains on. He was whistling and working, and this guy I was with was doing nothing but grumbling and grunting, and I just decided, right then and there, that I liked whistling better than I liked groaning and that I liked Bill a lot better than the guy I was dating.

74

I asked Bill to come to my high-school dance and he took me. We got going together. When he was dating me, he'd use his folks' car sometimes, and sometimes he'd hitch up some horses and he'd take the shortcut under the railroad pass and straight up to my place, and then we'd take my dad's car and go to the show. We had phones. They were party lines, and you didn't call each other up just to yak. Besides, I was twenty miles away, near Shullsburg, Wisconsin, and that was a long-distance call, because it had to go through Galena and Dubuque, Iowa, and all over. He called me a few times, if we had a date and he wasn't coming. I used to get letters from him. If he'd write on Tuesday, I'd get it on Thursday. We went together for a couple of years, and I was eighteen and he was twenty when we got married.

We were married in the parsonage in Schapville. We had eleven dollars between us. I had six and he had five, so I had controlling interest. It was September 19, 1934, and it was mud. Mud roads, mud everywhere. It was Friday when we were married, and we were back on Monday to go to work. Cutting corn, cutting corn fodder. Cutting it and making shocks, like they used to. In fact, Bill did that in the forenoon and we went and got married in the afternoon. Then we started out for my brother's the first night, because you couldn't stay in any hotels with the kind of money we had. We got going down that hill outside of Scales Mound, and the battery fell out of the car and all over that mud road. Bill just got out, whistled a bit, and put it back in the car.

The first year we came to the home place and lived with his folks and brothers. There was enough work, but there were too many people living in one house, and then his brother Elmer was getting married. One Sunday we took a walk over to the Hesselbachers', and he asked Bill to come and work for him. Bill said, "Well, when do you want me?" Clarence [Bill's brother] and Bill's parents were at the home place, and if Elmer was going to bring a wife, and there was

us, it was going to get pretty congested. So we went over to Hesselbachers'. It was one of those things, too, when you're living with your mother-in-law and you think, "Oh, I just got to get for myself." After you get for yourself, you realize what a grand old lady she was, how much you were really learning from her, that it was great living with her.

We worked for Hesselbacher for eight years. There were two houses over there, and we had one. But then we wanted to have a farm of our own, be independent. Then one day we were visiting the home place here, and Bill's dad was saying that he didn't want to keep the place any longer. Oh, there were things to build, things to do, and he said that he didn't feel like doing them anymore. He wasn't going to be using the place, so he figured he'd let the guy who wanted to build things to suit himself. He asked the boys if they wanted to buy it, and nobody did but Bill. They said to let Bill buy it, so he did. We moved in here. Grandpa lived with us for a while. Grandma had died while we were over at Hesselbachers'. We had worked hard there and we did here, too. Before we got modern and that, I always helped milk. In fact, if the men were out in the field, I could do the chores. I still do field work. Last year I disked 250 acres. Dorothy plowed furrow for furrow with Butch, I disked and harrowed, and Bill planted. That's the way we always went, and I always thought life was good to me.

Mildred said: *"They called her Aunt Emma. She was one of great-grandfather Bernhardt's daughters and she never married. She lived in Schapville. For more than thirty years she was church janitor and rang the bell at church. She thought it was her church. In her young days she'd work at housework, when they had young children. She was eighty-nine when she died. That was in 1961, while Butch was on his honeymoon."*

The home place - 1960

The house is over a hundred years old. Bill, Sr., was born in it—it was his father's house—and he bought it, added to it, raised his children in it. It is called "the home place." There is a place where one belongs, where one is at home. Every movement is a going away or a coming back. Some sadly search for a place to come back to. The Hammers do not have to. They have the home place. It binds them to each other, to the land, to life, to those who breathed and dreamed here and moved on. It is a place of comfort, of roots, of belonging. The sun throws the shadow of a windowpane into a cross on a breeze-stirred curtain and lends the house a symbol of sanctity. Pictures of George and Ida Hammer and their sons, resting on the time-cracked varnish of the family piano, seem to echo their presence. A doorway with etched glass reveals behind it decorative paper bells for Christmas. There are boxes with letters, souvenirs, and pictures. One picture is of Bill's parents and grandparents in front of the home place. The forms are not just utilitarian. They are sculpture, objects added with the times, re-minders of moments and years lived in this place, an art of accumulation. The stovepipe through the ceiling spells warmth; the window is an eye to the outside yard, through which the women watched their men and their children. What do they speak of—the child's chair, the soldier's picture on the wall, the books in the case, the globe of the world in the dining room? In a kitchen corner the old rural phone, now gone, rang to deaf ears except when the party number was yours. Long-distance operator: "TC Galena 815-834 Elizabeth. Hello, Elizabeth. My party wants Schapville 10, ring 2, Willis Hammer." Mildred would answer: "What, who? Can't hear. You coming out? Good! What say? The men . . . out . . . cold . . . pump frozen . . . they're fixing . . . come out . . . you got snowshoes? Ha-

ha, bring 'em!" Now there is direct-dial service. The telephone company did that, but they could not do anything about the weather; there are times when snowshoes are still needed. Texture of lace curtains, tablecloth, floral arrangement—look like art arranged to catch the side light, to please, to comfort. The old tractor covered in burlap, the chain hanging on the side of the barn, and next to it a nut on a nail (might be useful someday) now form a collage, unsigned, not yet assigned to a museum wall. "W.H." scratched into a barn side by a boy's penknife to make his immortal mark. In his bedroom, on his dresser, is his girl's picture. The wallpaper surrounds the room with the "jitterbugs" of another time.

MILDRED Bill always wanted this place. I think he grew up with the idea of being here, just like Jim [Bill, Jr.,'s son] is growing up with that idea, and like Junior did. When I first came here with Bill on dates, he used to talk of having it some day. He loved it. They were working the land with horses then, and he told me he would have black horses and black cattle, and maybe he was kidding when he said black sheep. I suppose he wanted it because the grandfather and the brothers were always here, and his mother and father.

Bill's mother—Ida Schiekoff was her maiden name—came from Germany to Canada to settle. His parents met as pen pals through a German paper they both read. They got to writing each other, and they did that for a long time. Bill's father, George, was living here. He bought the house, and his sister was caring for it. He went up to Canada to see Ida a couple of times, and they decided to get married. Then he brought her to this place.

Grandpa was pretty much of a stay-at-home. He had bad eyes and wore thick glasses. Nobody went around very much in those days, and he went even less than most people because he had a thing about those thick glasses. Grandma felt handicapped, too. She had a bad leg all her life. I guess that's what they got to be telling each other when they were writing—how each one was handicapped. Grandpa never did drive a car because of his eyes. Could never see

88

far enough. They doctored him all over when he was young. They even took him to Chicago when going there was like going to the edge of the world. He was very near-sighted, but he read a lot. He was a very well-read man. It was something when he read, because he'd hold the newspaper just a few inches away from his eyes.

They were church-going people. They went every Sunday when you had to go with horses, even when you had to use a sleigh. They never missed church. And their kids went too. It wasn't even a matter of making them go. Bill told me, "We were brought up that way. You just took it for granted you were going to church. Like going to school, you don't ask if you are or not, you just go."

I was wondering a while ago which would ever mean the most to Butch, the home place or the one he bought for himself. He told me that this place means more and that he'd lose that place down there before he'd want to lose this one. I understand that. It means to me, like if somebody'd say, "You can build a new house up on the hill and move up there," I'd have a lot of second thoughts. I've got my roots in this house. I don't know if I'd want to transplant up there on the hill. Antiques, the oldness of the house, don't mean anything to me, but I'd rather be here where I can see it like it was. Like when Janet was young and I'd see her run upstairs when she took a tantrum. Oh, how she could take a tantrum! "I'm mad at you..." Suppose I had a new house tomorrow. It would be like starting all over again. It's like a tree being planted somewhere. Plant a tree someplace and it's going to do a lot better and be happier there than if you take it after twenty years and transplant it. I'm happy here. But I could build a house on that hill and live up there if Jim was going to live here, because it would still be a Hammer that was here. That wouldn't hurt me.

We think that there is something special about this land out here. There are an awful lot of intelligent and great people you couldn't give this kind of life to. People have to pick their own life. We've got some smart people and they go out from Scales Mound and they go

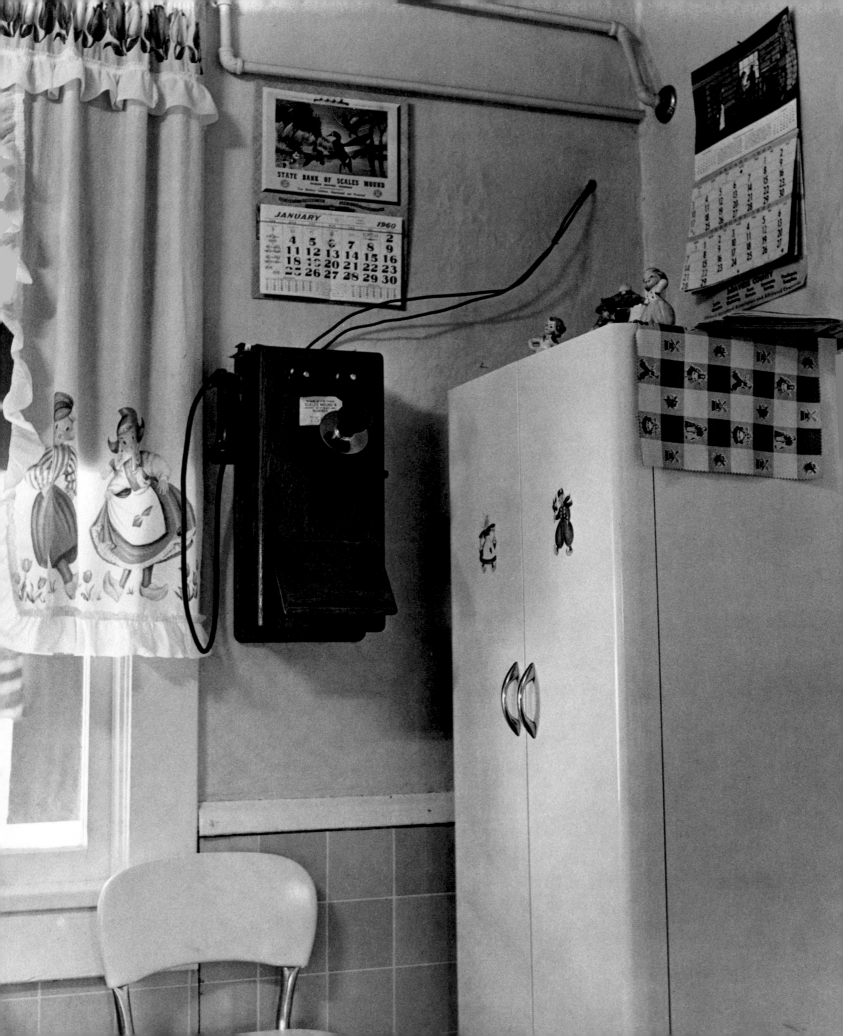

far in life. But I wouldn't want to trade with them. We worked and paid for this life ourselves. And it's not a backward place—only the commercialism and the golden tinsel haven't gotten here as bad as in a lot of places. According to today's standards, we're still squares and set in our ways, and I guess we still shock easier.

DOROTHY   Bill has his home place and I have mine. But, in a way, where Bill's folks live is a home place to me. I guess probably because it's where Bill used to live. We went there a lot. Practically every Sunday night I would go there with him while he did the milking. I got so I liked that place. It gives you a good feeling when you are there. You have a feeling that the Hammers have been there forever. Our kids like that place, and I think that they'll always think of it as Grandma's and Grandpa's. When we bought our place, the plan was that they'd retire to it and we'd take the home place. Now they're more for going to town. But Bill's father would have to have enough to do and it would be hard. He would have to come out to the farm, to keep busy, and that's why I think his dad won't ever fully retire.

BILL, JR.   Where I live is my home, but the home place is at my dad's. Some day, I'll be living there. Maybe it's more or less a habit. Sometimes, before I caught myself, I'd be heading for home and I'd wind up at the home place instead of going to where I live. So much of what I am is there. It's just that it's the Hammer place.... If things ever got rough, I'd hang on, I'd let everything go before this one, because it's the home place.

BILL, SR.   Just before Junior bought that place down there, we were going to quit here and let him have this. The more I got to thinking about it, the less I wanted to do it. It's pretty nice here. It's full of things to remember, more than new places you start someplace else. Maybe it's just changing things. I was born and raised here and I know there's something about it here. Maybe it's just because it's an old established neighborhood, or maybe the changes—its being built up more and the improvements over what it was—keep you here. But then, there've always been changes and we have to live with them. Mildred and I make lots of trips, short trips to friends in different states around here. You kind of dread leaving the house. You wonder whether you'll ever return or not. It's always nice to go, but I'm always interested to get back.

NEIGHBOR   You don't see that too much anymore, where a place will stay in the family for so many years. It amazes people around here.

THE HYMNAL

Schiller

Upright Grand

The forms mimic one another: the hymnal and the favorite songbooks on the piano, the monuments in the Hammer graveyard ("That's an old term; they call them cemeteries now") on a hill overlooking Mill Creek, the place where John Rudolph Hammer settled. Those forms merge with the silo, a symbol of fulfillment, of plenty, of life. That is the whole story. To sing and be happy; to toil on the land, subdue it, take sustenance from it; to return to it at the end of one's days; and to learn the cyclic nature of God's design.

The seasons demand recognition of the cycle of natural law. What person does not know this? But the farmer is engulfed by it, works with it. It is the pervasive element in his being. "Out here it's always changing. Each spring you start plowing and planting; then it grows; you harvest; then the land rests, and you use the things you grew to feed the animals; and then the spring comes again—it's a constant recycle."

My father, my son

They are called Old Bill and Young Bill. Nothing bad is meant by that—it is just what they are called. For most of his working life Old Bill has risen from sleep at 5:30 A.M. In the winter it is dark. He turns on the light in the home place and it spills out of the kitchen window onto the snow-covered ground. He milks, has breakfast, feeds the cows hay and silage, cleans out the dairy barn. By then it is time for noon dinner. In the afternoon there are chores to do, repairs to be made, another milking, and then supper. Young Bill has seen this all his life, was raised with it. It is part of what he saw and wanted to do.

BILL, JR.   "Never take out anybody you wouldn't want to marry." That was the main thing Dad told me, the one I remembered the most. That was all he ever said. Most of what he taught me he didn't say in words; it was through work and doing. He didn't say "Don't do this" or "Don't do that." He let me experiment a little. I'd just watch him to see how he did it, and some things I'd try to do the same way and added my own touch to it. Now he gives his opinion and I give my opinion, and we decide which is best. We never really fight. Some days he doesn't agree with what I'm thinking, and some days I don't agree with what he's thinking. Instead of blowing up at each other and saying a lot of things we don't mean, we give either one way or the other.

I always liked being with him. Getting to go along with him when I was small—that was fun. Going along and doing farm work was exciting because it was new. I used to bawl my head off when he went thrashing and I couldn't go, and that's the way it went till I was old enough to keep out of the way.

118

BILL, SR.   That must have been when he was about eight. Basically, what he says, I guess, was the feeling on both sides. What I mean is this: the idea of having a son who was interested in going and enjoyed doing the same thing was good.

BILL, JR.   As far as going out and playing games—baseball, or going fishing, or anything like that—we never did. It was the routine of doing the work and going along. Why, I'd be so proud if I got so I could load some bales, help him out! Then the next year I'd be that much older and then I could load half the load, and pretty quick I was loading the whole works!

BILL, SR.   That was when I liked it!

BILL, JR.   He was a good teacher. He'd tell me what to do—it was more like where to go—I wasn't old enough to realize what he wanted. He gave me freedom to make my own decisions as long as they were right. He'd correct me when I was wrong and gradually, each year, he'd give me more responsibility. If I'd do something wrong, he'd just tell me, "Well, do it the other way." He never did cuss much. If he ever cussed, you knew it was pretty bad.

BILL, SR.   I never could see getting all stewed up about something. I've seen the time when something'd happen and Junior would say, "Well, aren't you going to swear?" Well, no. What for? It wouldn't do any good.

BILL, JR.   Well, he'd correct you, and then after a few years you'd just automatically do it that way until you read a book and it comes up with new ideas. You might try it and, if it works, you graduate into that. He'd go along with new ideas. He knew from his own experiences with his dad that you can get too set in your ways and you can run into trouble. He knew the changes from his dad's time to

his time, and he knew things had to change. It'll be that way with Jim and me. The major things on the farm will be changed by the time I get old and Jim's working along. The difference between Dad and his dad is that when he took over the farm, he contoured this farm. His dad thought he was crazy to plow around the hills and make all those little strips. He was absolutely against it, wasn't he, pretty much?

BILL, SR.   Well, yes. Because, in the olden days, if you couldn't drive the horses straight, make a straight row of corn, you shouldn't be out there farming. That's the way they always did it. You could be proud. It was an old established theory that you got to drive straight. It should have been started sooner—to go around the hill. But I had a good relationship with my father even though I had three brothers. It was about the same as Junior and me.

BILL, JR.   I think your father was tougher on you than you were on me. If he said "Do it this way," you better do it that way. He was really the head of the household.

BILL, SR.   That generation was more headstrong. There's even a difference between Junior's generation and mine, or Junior's and Jim's. I've always tried not to stick to an old-fashioned idea if there was a better one around. Same as my father. What I mean is: he was willing to change. It may've taken a little talking or explaining to put across some new idea, but eventually he'd go along with it, like when tractors came in and when I wanted to contour-plow.

BILL, JR.   We've made changes. Like being partners. We own things together, and that allows us to make good use of the machines we own. That's the only way you could exist. We've still got the old machines, tractors. But we've got some new ones, too. If I had to own a complete

122

line and he had to own a complete line, we'd probably be so out of date that we'd barely survive. Like when we were milking two different places, we were both tied down. So we put the herd together, we milk in one place, and just divide things up. Now neither of us is tied down. When one wants to go away, he can while the other one does the work. Same equipment does us both the same job. But partnerships are rough. I might want to make changes that he might not think are right; he might be doing something I don't like, but you've just got to work it out. It doesn't always come out even, but you've got to give one way or the other. Here's where our relationship has always been pretty good: one doesn't expect the other guy to do more than one does. If he milks five nights a week, he doesn't begrudge it if I'm not milking, and I don't begrudge it that he isn't milking when I am. If we go out to drive stakes and I drive fifty steel stakes and he doesn't, well, fine! I don't feel that I'm doing more than he. He's doing something on his share. Might be two different things we're doing, yet we're both working for the same thing. Neither of us will go to town and play when the other's home working. When there's something to be done, we both do it. Neither one of us will leave the other one alone.

We've got our own rules. There might be a set of rules for a partnership, but some of ours aren't like those rules. Like when I had a third of what he owned in land, and I was still getting half of everything. Working with anybody else, that would be altogether wrong. That's my advantage in working with my father. That's what I mean by our own rules. The same way as me farming. I could never go farming if it wouldn't be for him. Why should he stick his neck out for me? He could just stay with his land and say, "The heck! I can make a living. You go make your own!" But he didn't. When I started farming, he signed notes and stuck his neck out for me. I could have gone down and taken him and all his years of hard work with me.

I've learned a lot from him. I guess in some ways we think the

same. Like we'd sooner buy a piece of machinery and have it than have custom work done. I like to have new stuff, but if it's going to drive me insane paying for it and worrying about where the money is going to come from, I'd just as soon go along with my old things and be done with it. I've learned from him and we've always been on good terms. You can pick your friends but not your relatives. I'm glad I got him. Because it doesn't matter what you do, or where you go, a father and a son are always related. It's better to be on good terms. But we never thought about it; it just comes naturally. I can't say he really ever bossed me. I'd say he led the way, more than what I realize.

BILL, SR. It's good to have a son. It's something that every father wants. When he was born, I thought it was great. I liked having the girl first, for the simple reason that there were no girls in our family. But I sure wanted a boy, too. I hoped he would like farming. I wanted to give him all the opportunity in the world to try something else. I sure liked it when he decided to do farming. And I liked it when she named him Hammer, Jr. He's a good farmer. That takes a lot. You have to be up-to-date, you have to be fairly well educated, these days, and you have to be ambitious, not afraid to put in long hours, and versatile. And you've got to be able to give credit to God. He is the Father of us all, of everything. I would say that we farmers realize that more than anybody, because you can make a lot of materials but it's impossible for any human being to do without the help of God what we farmers do.

You might need His help when you have children, too. With Junior, I wouldn't know of any problems. We haven't had any serious disagreements. I tried to tell him right from wrong and it must have been all right because he turned out all right. We tried to bring him up in religious surroundings. And I think that a father could try to live as an example. Tell the children, and live that way, and I think

126

they will follow in your footsteps more than you'd think. At the time you don't realize that things you do are making any impression, until you get older. But that isn't all of it either. There's been some very good fathers and the sons haven't turned out that way. What's the truth? You're lucky if they turn out good. If they do, they do. I don't think you have to be talking and lecturing. You just do. I think it's a very good way of doing it.

I was paying a lady in a store in town when Butch came in, and she said, "I see you have the boss with you today, again." I said, "Well, I very seldom go very far without him," and she said, "You know, that's what I always liked and admired about you two. You get along so well, you're always together, and you're always working together." Now, she lives in Elizabeth. Where did she get the idea from? She really doesn't know anything about how we get along. Where does it show, where does it crop out? Just the same, it's a good feeling when you hear things like that.

JIM HAMMER, AGE 10   I know what it takes to be a farmer. He's a man who's strong, a man who can think, make decisions quick, and all that. A man like my dad.

The wedding–May, 1961

After a three-year courtship of going to movies in Dubuque and Galena, to basketball games, of swimming in farm ponds, driving out to look at the Mississippi River, strolling through fields, working hard to build up to the time for the wedding, Bill and Dorothy were married in the First Presbyterian Church of Scales Mound. It was May 6, 1961. It was also May 6, a few years before, when Dorothy followed Bill out of town, stopped him at Brickners', and they started going together.

MILDRED   When Junior was getting married, I guess I thought of my own wedding. I guess every time you hear of a wedding you think of your own. You listen to the vows and you wonder if you've ever broken any of them. I was very happy about that wedding. He was getting a good girl. She was a girl in the neighborhood and she got a lot of honors in school. I always told her that I was proud of her, that I thought she did great. I bought a graduation present for Dorothy. I wouldn't have done it, the way I did, for anyone else in the world. I was in Aurora and I saw this dress and I said, "That looks like Dorothy!" She wears the same size as Janet. I thought, "Should I buy it for her or shouldn't I?" There was only one of them and I thought, "Yep, I'm going to buy it for her."

I remember the day Dorothy was born. I remember asking Celia what she was going to name her, and I remember her saying, "Dorothy." I saw her grow up. People didn't go out much then, but we were both Presbyterians. Her family belonged to one church and we went to the other. When the two churches would get together, we'd always see them. As the children grew up, we shared the same things. We had a very open relationship about our kids—what our kids should do and what we were going to allow them to do. We had a wonderful understanding. Like she'd say, "I sent your son home." I'd say, "I wanted you to." Or she'd say, "Our kids are mad at me," or I'd say, "Our kids are mad at me."

Junior and Dorothy had a long-range plan to get married. They didn't rush into it. She graduated high school and went to work, and they were talking about the next year. Then he said, "Well, we've got to start making plans." The summer before they were married he gave her a diamond, so we knew it was coming. He took extra work up at the school to buy her diamond and, like he said, "It doesn't have to be the biggest in the world, but I don't want them to have to look and look to see it either." On the day he married Dorothy I thought it was the smartest thing he ever did, because I just liked her and thought he made the right choice. I think we are good friends. I hope she thinks we are.

DOROTHY   He never really asked me. We just talked about when we would get married. Setting the date, that took quite a bit of doing. He wanted to get married in April, before the corn planting. I didn't want to before May or June. We finally settled on May, between the oats and the corn. I guess I had some inkling then that I was going to be a farmer's wife.

Marrying Bill was the next step after going together. We went together, we knew we loved each other, we knew we wanted to be together. The next thing, in that day, was to get married; not just go live together. So we got married and on our honeymoon we drove to California. We didn't stay as long as we planned; we came right back here. We do that all the time when we take trips; we can't wait to come back. It's so unreal to be gone. That's the unreal world. We know where life begins and ends here. Life goes on here. It's nice to think about going away and doing, getting away from it, but it's always nice to get back to life that really is. When I think about it, it was like a wasting of time. Our real life was back here. We wanted to get back and start living. All I ever thought about being married was that it's going to be great, you're going to be with him all the time.

BILL, JR. I suppose it would have been nice to have a June wedding. But that's too much of a season for crops, and I can't be running off and getting married. That's why we weren't taking much of a honeymoon, and we had our home here and we hadn't lived in it yet. The trip was fantasy—well, it was real, too—but I mean, it just wasn't our life to be traveling around. We stayed a couple of days out there and then drove right back. I mean, it all was new. I was thinking about our future. I was used to my own way. It's quite a change to be married. Everybody's scared of change, whatever it is. But I thought she wanted to get married and I loved her and wanted to share my life with her.

Dorothy and Bill had bought a 10-by-48-foot trailer and parked it in the yard next to the home place. That was to be their home, and they moved their things into it. On Friday, the day before their wedding, Bill was still getting things together. Mildred helped him pack for his honeymoon. She handed him a freshly ironed shirt. Afterward Dorothy would be doing that for him. That morning, as all mornings did, started early for Bill and his father. By dawn light they carried buckets of feed, did chores and some field work. After that Bill, Sr., went back to the kitchen and ate one of the muffins Mildred had baked for next day, when there would be company. Ken Hickman, Dorothy's father, had a bit of bad luck: one of his cows died. That afternoon Bill went to Dubuque, picked up the formal wedding clothes, and got a haircut. That night he drove over to the Hickmans' and down their road. He looked down that road, his car lights flooding it, and at the house and thought, "Well, this is the last time I'll be coming for her like this." They went over to Scales Mound High School and watched the promenade at the Junior dance.

On Saturday the men in the bridal party gathered at Janet's house. Brickner was best man and helped Bill dress. When they left the house and walked down the path in single file, they could see in the distance the valley of the home place. Since those times, Brickner has worked hard and modernized his house so that you would hardly recognize it today. At the church were an organist and a singer; Brenda, the daughter of Bill's sister, Janet, was the flower girl. Dorothy's best friend and Dorothy's sister were the bridesmaids. After the bridal couple made their vows, after their kiss, after the reception line at the church, everyone went over to the Flamingo Tea Room, where the elder Hammers had celebrated their twenty-fifth anniversary. After having cake, ice cream, and punch, Bill and Dorothy went back to her father's house to change their clothes. When they got out of the car, they walked along the same path of the field as they had when Bill was courting her. It seemed as if things were being repeated.

BILL, SR.   KENNETH HICKMAN

FLAMINGO TEA ROOM

Dorothy is pregnant— January, 1962

Spring, summer, fall—those seasons had passed. Now it was winter. It had been a good year for the crops and for Bill and Dorothy. Their life had really begun, they had settled into marriage in the ways they were raised to. Their hopes were for the child she carried. At thirteen Bill had prophesied that his firstborn would be a son. Now they waited for the prophecy to be fulfilled. Dorothy had taken a job and Bill worked with his father. The trailer sheltered all their early married life.

When the land lies fallow, covered with snow, the bite of winter is the main thing. The animals rely entirely on the Hammers for their feed, and out of the silos and the barns comes the harvest of the year. That winter at the home place, the trailer parked next to it, the Hammers enjoyed the warmth of it, and being together. Sheltered from the icy darkness of the Midwest's long winter nights, their stiff bodies recovered from the frozen grip of the day. They rested in the living room, read, and watched T.V.; there was not much talking. Some evenings they all gathered in the kitchen while the women baked.

DOROTHY We liked the trailer. It was our first home. We had so many things we couldn't have had otherwise—a modern kitchen, lots of built-ins and closets. It was like living in a small house. I was working. I worked probably six months, in Dubuque. Then I had to quit. Bill was doing the thing he likes best, farming. We were busy with work and thinking about names. I thought it would be a boy—I hoped it would be a boy. We used to go through name books, names for boys and names for girls. Bill always liked the name "Jim." He couldn't see having a Willis Hammer III.

158

BILL, JR. I was thinking positive. I always do that until things go opposite. I really wanted to have a boy as my first, but as long as it was healthy, I wouldn't be dissatisfied. I wasn't the first and I always considered the advantages of that. I always thought the son should be older and the girl should be younger. But we were young then, and I don't think when you're that age you realize all the things you should. I was too young to know what having a baby really meant. My idea of marriage at that time was a lot different from what it is today. I know I loved her more when she was carrying the baby than when we were going together; and I love her more today than the day I married her.

One cold Saturday, Mildred bundled herself and some of the sumptuous food for which she is noted into the pickup and went to Janet's house. Janet was giving Dorothy a baby shower, and pinned a corsage on Dorothy that she had made of ribbon bows and diaper pins. The women sat in a square around the room. The talk was of cooking, the men, the weather, sewing, and the kind of Hammer that Dorothy was going to bring into their lives.

169

The women

There is men's work and there is women's work. There is a lilt to it when the women say, "The men are out in the field" or the men say, "The women are in the kitchen." It means that this is the way the work gets divided—another way of belonging to the original plan.

MILDRED   Maybe it's just old-time talk. There was one farmer around here that when he wanted his wife he'd holler: "Hey, woman!" Even our hired hand, when he wanted me, instead of calling me by name, he'd stand out in the yard and holler: "Hey! Woman!"

Even in the wedding vows it says that she should be his helpmate. I think that a man should be the head of the house. I hate to see a man run by a woman. I think it goes back to the Bible. It's a religious understanding. That's the way the work gets divided: this chore's yours and that chore's mine.

I'd rather be a woman than a man. I'd rather do women's work than men's work. I guess it's instinct. I'd rather cook, do the gardening and yard work, and raise chickens. It's just a way of life that women inherit that work. With most farm wives it's the same way, at least with the happy ones it's that way: helping out wherever they see a place to do things and knowing how to do them. Being a good helpmate is not having to do it, but being able to do it, if he's sick or if he's not here. There's no competition; it's working together. I help in the field and I scrub the milk house and polish it from one

176

end to the other. It wouldn't come easy to a man to do the polishing and waxing. They don't have the time, anyhow. They take care of getting rid of the manure and I take care of getting rid of the spots on the stainless steel. I guess there's where women's work and men's work comes in. Like the chickens: Junior just hates to care for chickens, hates the job. He would just do away with them. He wouldn't feed a chicken if his life depended on it—he hates chickens! He says women who want chickens should take care of them. If we go away and I want my chickens to be cared for, I get Jim to do it. Now Jim says he doesn't like them and, just like his dad, he'll tell you, "That's women's work."

I've always loved the farm. I don't even look forward to retirement. I'd like to stay on the farm when I retire. I guess if you fall in love with a man, and you get married to him, it's mostly being with him and helping him that counts. I don't know if I am just so dependent on him or my family. I could live anywhere with them. I can't picture living anywhere without them. I could live anywhere, or do anything, with Bill. A farm wife better like what she's doing, or she's going to be awfully unhappy. I like what I'm doing and I don't want to do anything else.

They're talking about women's liberation. I don't understand it. It goes right over my head, but it doesn't affect me one way or the other. I'm busy living one day at a time and being me. I never felt that I wasn't liberated. Bill and I are free. I can't make him feel or think the way I think, and he has no right to make me feel the way he feels, to any extent. Suppose I like to read and he doesn't, or I want to go somewhere and he doesn't. Well, I don't make him read or go. But he doesn't make me stay home or stop me from reading either. We never had any wrong feelings in that way. We just help each other in any way we can. I've always felt needed.

There were those years when I worked away from home. I was working to improve the standard of living. Those were some of the

rough years when my nerves needed a change. We needed cash. Junior was getting into cars, Janet was getting married, and we needed some new machinery. I'd go to work in the morning and everything would be just fine. I'd come home at night and maybe it wasn't so fine, but I would pretend it was. I stayed there longer than I thought I would, because there was always this and that we needed. I look on those years like when someone serves in the army. I didn't enjoy it, but it was an experience. I had never been away from home before. Now that it's all over, it's all right. I was awful glad the day I could quit and come home to stay.

I enjoyed the whole thing of my life, the work and the kids, the way it went. I think every man wants a son and every woman does, too. We got both kinds that we wanted, a son and a daughter. My relationship with Junior was come and go; he was mostly his dad's. He was always out there with his dad. Janet and her dad were real close, too. In the high moments of his life I always knew Junior liked me more than he let on. You'd hear him bragging how Mom made this and how Mom made that and he'd go to a picnic and tell them, "That's my mom's potato salad." I think we were as close as most sons and mothers are. He's often thought I was awfully strict. I enjoyed it all, his growing up, just watching the aggravation of him and how he'd work things out. He'd get provoked at me for being concerned about him. Sometimes he'd run away because the other kids would call him "chicken" if he wouldn't. He'd just go for the day, or do things like that, and I'd have to punish him. Bill would leave it to me. He doesn't like to fight. He'd say, "Wait till your mother catches you, wait till your mother sees what you did!"

I was always telling Junior to keep good company. There are always good and bad everywhere; some of the good are worse than you think, and some of the bad are better than you think. We have more good than bad around here. There's not much drinking around here. Speeding cars were my big worry. But, it was never any big problem with him, raising him. It was just a boy fighting to be a man. He didn't want to work in the garden with me or rake the yard; that was for women. He had an aversion to being called a sissy. When he was about ten years old he said, "Now you stop calling me Billy; you make me sound like a sissy when you call me Billy. You call me Butch. It makes me sound tough." He always tried to be a man and do for himself. When he went to town school, they made it rough for him the first few years. We weren't even supposed to know about that. He'd say, "I'm going to town school. I got there and I'll handle my own troubles."

I was born in Wisconsin—just across the line—on a farm. I went to a country school and I loved it and the kids. I've always been on a farm. My folks were renters. They rented until they saved money, eleven thousand dollars or so, and they thought they were rich. They invested it, up there, in a farm there was supposed to be a mine on. Then, suddenly, the Depression hit. The mine closed and they lost the farm. Then we lived on our doctor's farm, and Dad worked on that fifty-fifty shares. I lived there until I married Bill. The folks lived there until they retired.

My maiden name was Evans. I don't know when the Evanses came to this country. They were Welsh, though. I was a tomboy when I was a kid, I had horses, I loved all that stuff that boys did. When Mom made me weed in the garden, that was punishment. Tears would run down my cheeks and I'd say to her if she loved me she wouldn't make me do this. I started milking cows when I was six years old—you're old enough to go to school, you're old enough to milk cows. My older sisters and brothers spoiled me. There were three ahead of me, and then for eight years there were none born until I was; four years after me they had another boy. I can never remember a grandparent except that my grandpa was always sick, and I can remember his funeral, but I can't remember ever being with him. My grandpa had a second marriage; that was my father's stepmother. We never called her Grandma, we called her Aunt Jen. He was Grandpa, but she was Aunt Jen.

My father was kind of like Bill. He never flew off the handle. My mother was kind of like me. I never realized it until after she was gone. My mother was strict and she was a worrier. Dad would set out whistling and she'd be cussing. I didn't realize until afterwards, either, how hard my mother worked and worried and my dad whistled. It's easier to whistle than to work and worry. He whistled and whittled. Bill sings and whistles, but he works very hard. I guess my dad did, too, in a way, but not as hard as Bill works. My dad was fun to live with. He was a good kind dad, always sympathetic with you, hardly ever raised his voice to us. When he did, if he just called you a darn fool, you'd know that you really had it. My dad taught me to square-dance. Mom didn't dance, so I was his dancing partner. We danced at neighborhood parties. You'd clear the stuff out of a room and have a party; everybody would dance. Oh, how I loved that, dancing with Dad.

When I was a teenager I never did think about what I was going to do. What does any sixteen-, seventeen-, or eighteen-year-old girl think about? Boys. At that time I didn't think much about whether they were Catholic, Protestant, farmers, city boys, or what, just so they were boys. It didn't matter until Bill came along. Then, when I came down here with Bill, I loved the country. I liked his parents and I liked the place here. I went home praising it to my folks, how nice it was.

If there is anything lacking in my marriage, it might be that most of the time I was the old witch. Bill's the head of the family, and the kids and I respect him. Bill doesn't like trouble, and that left it to me to say whether they couldn't or could do something when he'd tell them to ask me. "Dad says I can go if you say I can go." That left it to me. I think it worked out all right. When they grew up, they didn't think that I was much of an ogre.

I've always been glad that I was with Bill. I like being a woman.

DOROTHY   I learned a lot from Millie. She knows how to do so many things. Like cooking. She can make something from nothing and it's really great. I learned a lot from her that I don't even realize. She always made me feel at home. When I went there—and even now—I'd ask her if there was something I could do, and she'd tell me and I'd go do it. She didn't have me sit in the corner; I always took part. Any time you go there you take part, and it makes you feel like you're one of them. You don't realize at the time what you've learned and how much of an impact it had on your life.

I found that with my mother, too. I felt a lot closer to her after I was married. I didn't appreciate her until I found out what it meant to be a mother and a wife, especially if you live on a farm. She's the helping hand and a partner. But I'd rather be the woman than the man. I couldn't take some of the pressure that he takes. He looks at the years and he's got payments to make and he's got seeds and fertilizer—and you name it—to buy; and he knows his cows aren't milking like they should, and he knows that he's not going to have the money from that, and the hog prices might go down, and he has to wonder where the money is going to come from. I worry about it, yes, but I always figure he'll take care of it. I mean, he always does.

BILL, JR.   That's more or less the way it is. There's women's work and there's men's work. She should just get along with him, be backing him instead of fighting him, and have respect for him. But that will go in city life or any life. If your wife loses respect for you, you're in trouble. And the man's work is making a good enough living to keep your wife respecting you.

Jim is born

As Bill, Sr., says: "Rockefellers have heirs. We just have sons." James Alan Hammer was born February 13, 1962. He was the firstborn son and grandson. From the beginning of time that has been special.

Coming home from the hospital, Bill and Dorothy got in their car, took a proud look at Jim, and drove to her folks' place. There her mother and brother peeked in. In the background was the landscape of their courting days and of the day in May when Dorothy was married and walked along the field in her wedding dress. It was a ritual of homecomings for Jim. In the trailer, beside the home place, Jim lay in his cradle, his parents and his grandmother Mildred admiring him. While Dorothy nervously looked at Jim's hand, Bill stretched in pride and accomplishment. In the barn there were new lambs, and Bill saw to them. He was happy.

DOROTHY   Jim was the first baby I'd really ever seen. When I realized it was mine, I thought "My heavens!" Bill, I guess, was the thrilled one, because he saw him immediately after he was born. I can't remember what he said. I think I was pretty foggy at the time. He probably didn't say much; the doctors and nurses were still in the room. He probably just smiled a lot—he's very smiley. It was after midnight. Then he left and went home and I didn't see him until the next night, but he had sent flowers and the card had on it "Thanks for the boy."

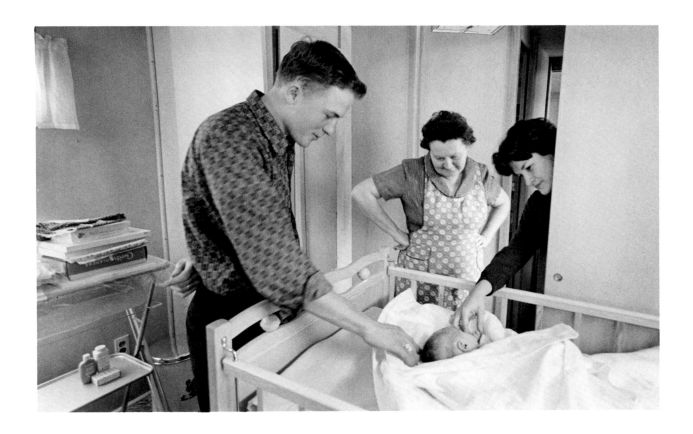

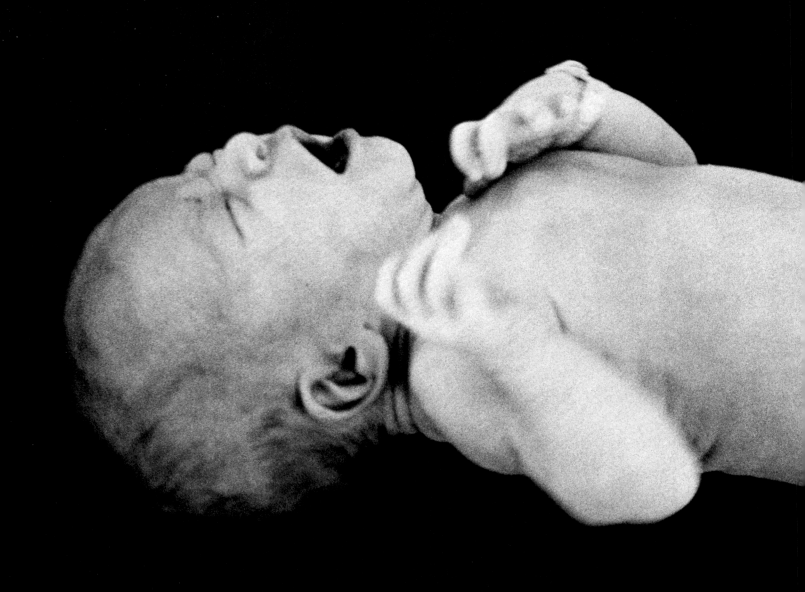

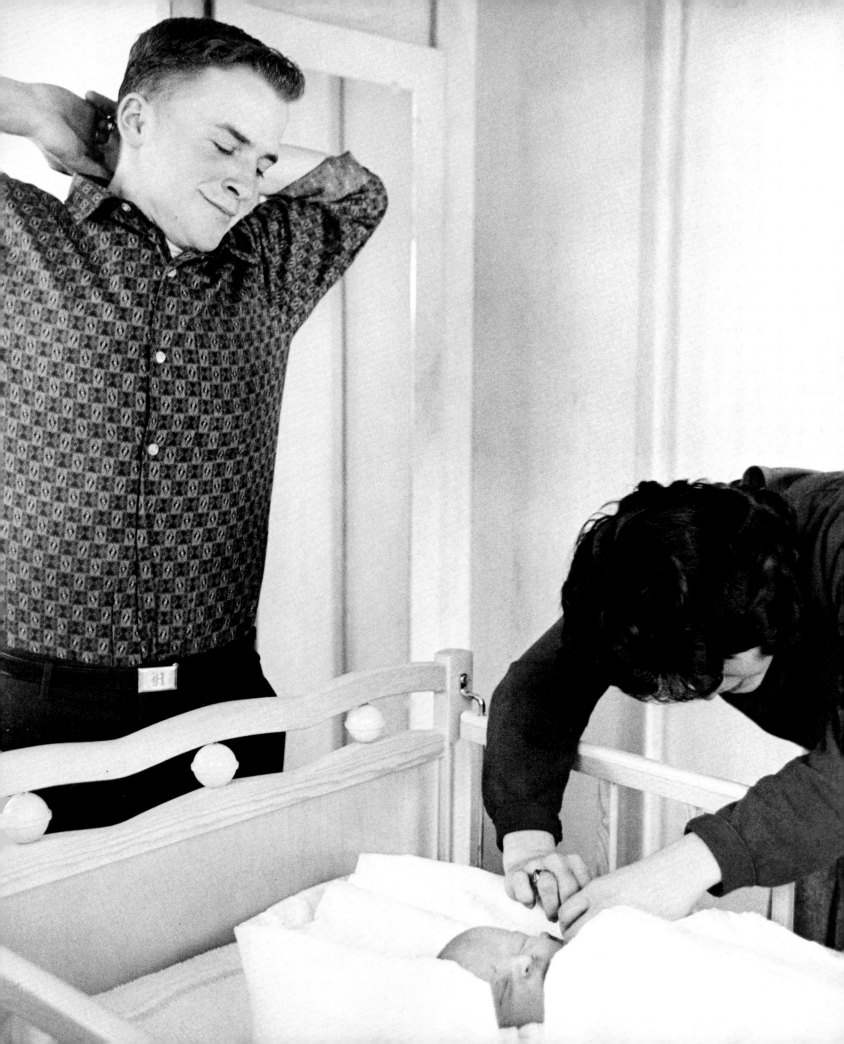

Jim was the first grandson for both our parents. They thought it was great. When my parents came up to the hospital to see me, they had a whole list of names. They knew we had figured on James Alan, but we weren't all that sure. They brought a white sheet with all fantastic names on it. First was Willis Arthur Hammer III, and James Alan, and a few crazy names thrown in, but they pretty well knew it was going to be Jim. Their name wasn't anywhere. My brother had thrown in Herbert Hubert. Herb, after my grandpa.

It was a nice day when we brought him home. We were lucky he came before the bad snow storm. The snow was pretty deep then, but they were expecting more, the blowing kind where you're trapped in. A friend of ours called and said that if I had to go anywhere he'd plow the way ahead of us. So we weren't too worried. After we got him home we had a bad snow storm. The afternoon that we came home Janet came over and stayed with me, because Brickner, Bill, and his dad went over to a farm sale.

That's another thing. When you see a farm that looks like it should have made it, made a good living, and then you see someone sell it and go off to do something else, you wonder how you're going to do it. It was getting worse at that time. There were a lot more people going out of farming. I think that year—and maybe the next or so—made you think, "Is there really that much of a future for a young man to start now?" There were high expenses and we didn't have much. The factory job that Bill got helped. It worked out right for us.

BILL, JR. On the day I brought her to the hospital I didn't do much. We left early in the morning for Cuba City—that's in Wisconsin—where the hospital is. I waited all day until about a quarter after twelve that night. I had quit work and, when that was over, I came home and resumed the work. It was mostly chores, and Dad filled in and did them himself, milking, cleaning out the barn, feeding silage. It wasn't haying or harvesting, so Jim was born at a pretty good time. But every day on a farm is busy. We don't really have a lax season. We work just as hard in the winter time as we do in the summer time. When it's cold, it may be harder. You've got water that's frozen-up or a tractor that won't start or, if an animal breaks out, there's a fence to fix. You might not get the volume of work, but you're working so much longer for the little work that you are doing. When I saw Jim for the first time he was in pretty rough shape, but I liked the looks of him. I never liked the looks of babies, but your own you do. I liked him. Cute. To some people he probably wasn't, but to me he was. I was happy. I called everyone to let them know.

I was thinking about him being a farmer, same as Dad and me. But I felt the same way as Dad did, and still do, that Jim is going to have to find his own way. If Jim wants to be a farmer, fine! And I'll try to help him, too. He'll have to try something else, too, before he can make sense out of the whole situation. I've had a lot of other jobs.

194

Tried being a factory worker, worked in a mine, things like that. I didn't like it, so I was sure that farming was what I wanted. You've got to have the opportunity to try something else to be sure about farming. It takes a lot of things to do it well.

Jim's going to have more education than Dad and I did. Dad had an eighth-grade education, I had a high-school education, Jim's going to have a college education or a degree in agriculture. Farming's getting so complicated. You have to be a veterinarian, a soil scientist, you have to have production, you have to be in so many fields when you're a farmer; you have to get better all the time just to survive. Today there are so many diseases that there weren't when Dad was starting. The land is crowded now. You're raising more animals on less space. Once, if you raised a hundred head of pigs, you'd have no problem with disease, because sometime during the year you could let that land be sitting idle. When it sits idle, and the sun hits it, it automatically purifies itself. You could change pastures then, but now you have to use your land all the time—all of it—because you have to produce more, and so you put pigs in the same place where there were pigs before. If the first bunch had a disease, then the next bunch will have it. So you have to know about those kinds of things, about drugs and vaccinations, how to prevent disease and how to use the land. Years ago on a farm, it was a matter of how hard you worked, how well you did. If you put in long hours and worked hard you'd be considered a top farmer. Not any more. It's what you know, not only what you do. We won't urge Jim necessarily to go on to college, but something that will help with whatever he's going to do or whatever he wants to be. But if he goes to college and decides on becoming a farmer, he'd better have the talent for it, too. We had some college-educated farmers that came out here and they went broke. Whatever the future has, he'd have the farm just the same and he'd have to make the changes just the same as we had to do.

At a farm auction, Old Bill and Young Bill purchased the remnants of a farm going out of business: it was a sad thing. That afternoon, in the late light of a coming storm, Bill stopped chores and contemplated the future. Now that he had a son he would work harder than ever so that his place would never be auctioned off. Then it was black night. The lights of the home-place kitchen, seen from the trailer, cookie-cut the window out of the darkness. Old Bill sat at the kitchen table feeling secure. He said of that time:

"I was very happy to think—call it pride, conceit, whatever you want—that there was another Hammer. Well, he's a Hammer. In the immediate family, he's the only Hammer boy to carry on the name."

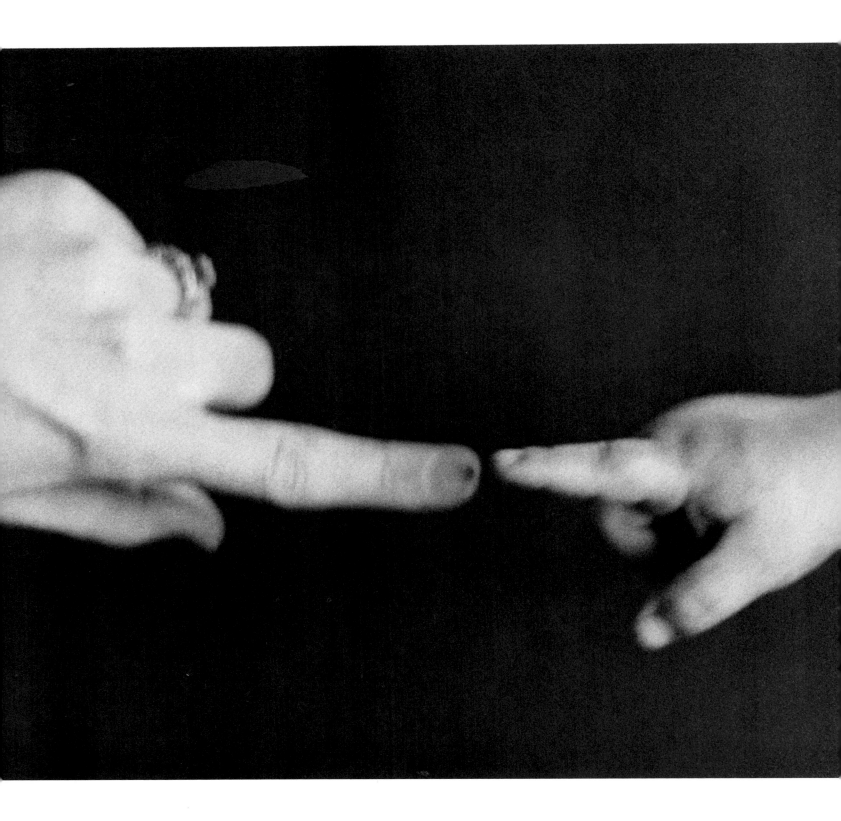

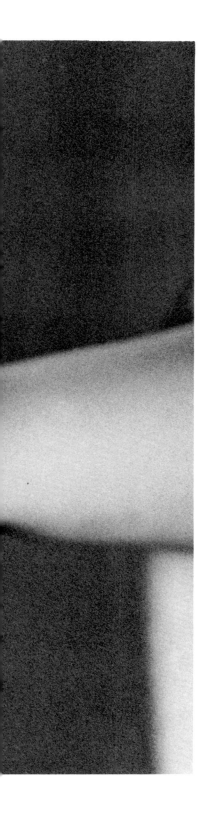

The gift–January, 1964

In a month Jim would be two. In 1963, the day after Christmas, his sister Judith was born. If he gained any more weight, Dorothy and Bill used to quip, they would not be able to pull him around in his wagon. The past year had been busy. Dorothy had been raising one child and having another. She also baked her own breads and cakes, sewed her own dresses and clothes for her family, worked in her garden, and canned food. Like Mildred, she helped with the men's work: she baled hay, drove the tractor, and cleaned milking machines. When the men were not eating Mildred's huge noontime dinner at the home place, Dorothy enjoyed preparing it. The men never had a weight problem, and the meat, potatoes, creamed corn, string beans, brown gravy, Jell-O, salad, bread pudding, fresh butter, hot rolls, jam and honey, fruit drink, milk, coffee, pie, and ice cream suited them well. Janet and Dorothy had combined their efforts in a small, part-time but busy sewing business.

For fun, in the summer Bill would trailer their fifteen-foot boat to the Mississippi and they would fish and water-ski. Sometimes they had friends in and some Saturday nights they went dancing at the Royal Palais, a dance hall in Galena. When Bill played tournament basketball with the town team, Dorothy would go along and watch.

They had rented the Siskas' land, which adjoined the Hammer fields, and in November they moved their trailer home down there, next to the farmhouse, across the road from the abandoned, weather-beaten, one-room school that Bill had attended. They had eighteen cows of their own and, with the landowner's, Bill was milking thirty. 1963 had been a good year, and now with the cold of January, they longed to get on with the work of spring and summer. In the meantime, Jim was receiving some gifts from his mother, who thought, "It sure seems like it's been a long winter."

DOROTHY   Jim started walking at Christmas, just before his first birthday, and he could say "Daddy," "Mommy," and "Thank you." He also said "No," and he knew just what that meant. I spent a lot of time with Jim and it was fun teaching him. I'd show him how to count. I'd show him how to hold up one finger and keep the rest down. You teach them that and a lot of little things you don't even think about, from tying shoes to dressing, combing hair, brushing teeth—all those things—little things, but you've got to learn them. Because she's

212

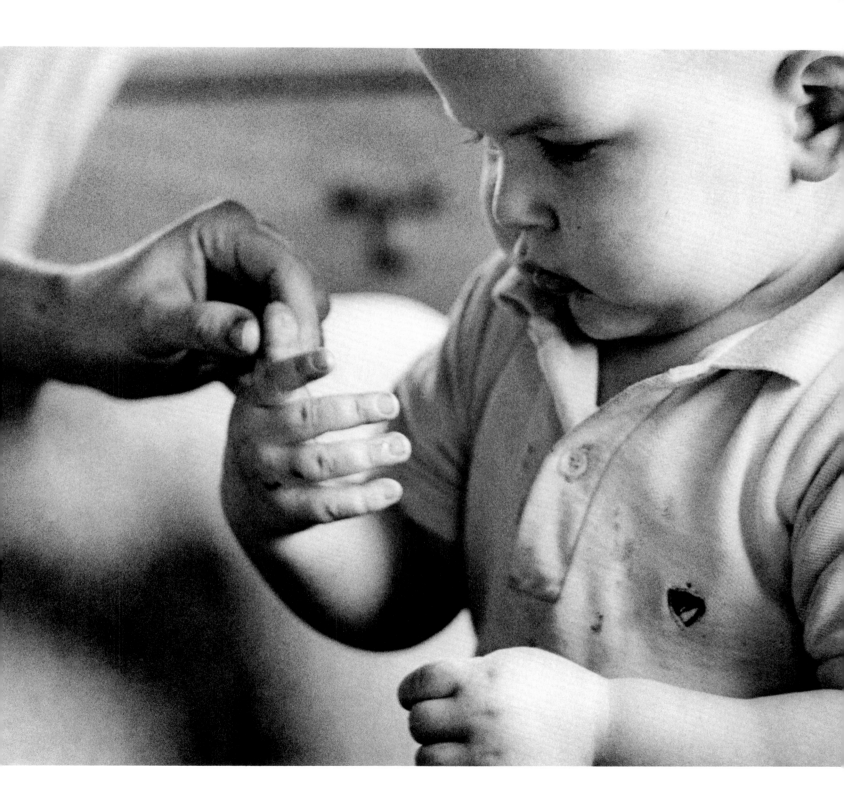

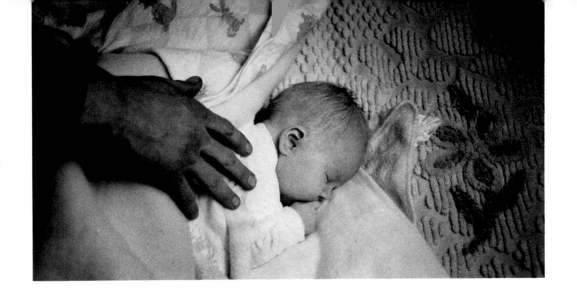

around, you learn them from Mother. But while she's doing that, she's teaching other values. She's giving them, I think, a sense of home and family, security in the family. Bill says he learned from his mother how to be civilized, or try to be. He thinks it's important for a mother to show kids she loves them by reading stories, spending time with them. But maybe it's all instinct. Mildred believes that about mothers. She says it is a matter of instinct, protection, and being proud. She was laughing when she said, "You look at your child and you say, 'Look what I've done—I've got to protect it.'" I think she meant it. And she's been a real good mother.

Jim

On a hot day in August, 1964, Jim, with his hair cut short and a smile on his dumpling face, took off on important business. He chased a cat; in his father's car he tried to assert himself, lost, and then walked hand in hand with Bill to see a quarry blast. He looked at Judy in her playpen and played with some neighbor children in the barnyard. At the home place he listened to a chicken cackle and saw an old sow nursing her young. He watched Bill climb the silo and said, "When I get big like Dad, I'll do that, too."

DOROTHY   Jim started going places with Bill just as soon as he was able to walk and run well. He even went when he couldn't. He'd fall down, he'd get up and try again. So Bill would take him and set him in front of him on the tractor. He wanted to be with Bill all the time. Jim's not too crazy about his sisters. He wanted a brother; I would've liked another boy. He's got too much responsibility. I mean, Bill was the only Hammer boy of his father. That makes Jim the only Hammer boy. You expect more of him. Jim likes the idea. So he'd watch Bill milk and do chores, and he'd play and he'd be learning. He was getting to be a Hammer, all right.

At Thanksgiving they had sold the trailer and moved into the farmhouse. It had nine rooms, a new bathroom, running water, and a wood-burning furnace. It and 190 acres belonged to the Siskas, a Chicago family. Bill and his father managed it for them. Dorothy took a job. Several days a week she left Jim and Judy with Mildred and drove five miles to a factory located on a 500-acre farm. There she worked an eight-hour shift putting new diamonds and sapphires into old phonograph needles. To Bill and Dorothy it was only the beginning of what seemed like an endless struggle to keep themselves down on the farm.

216

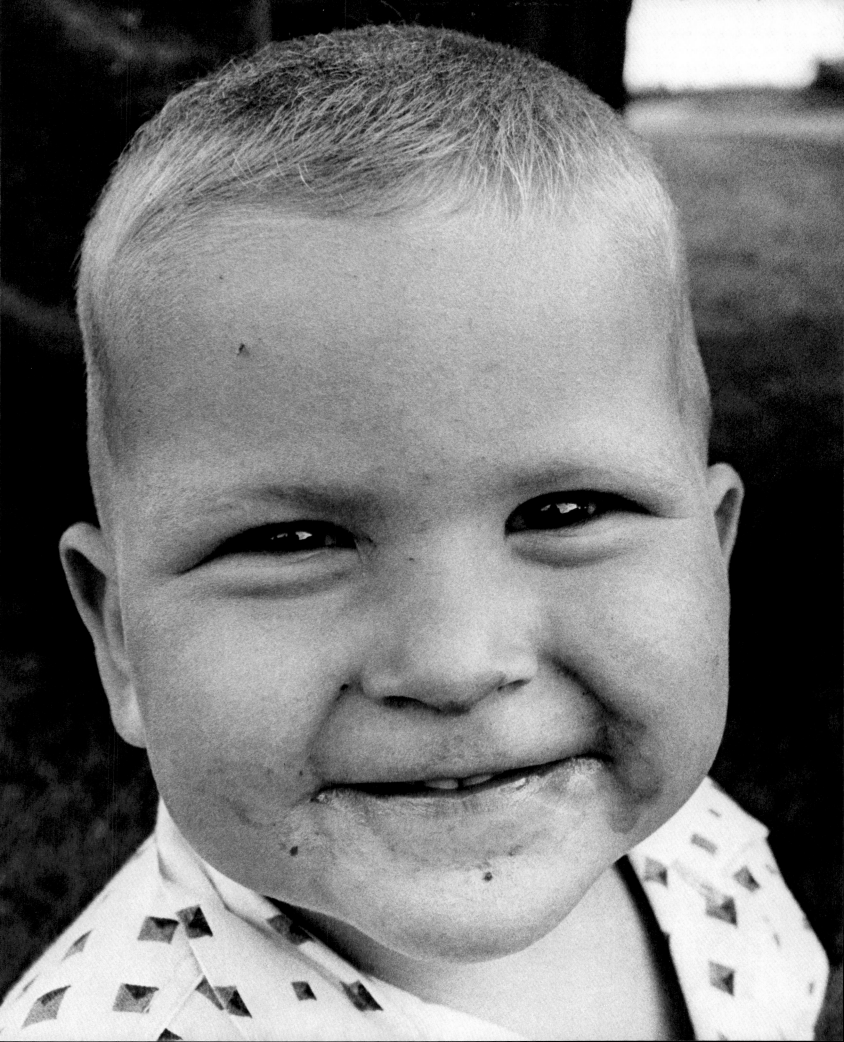

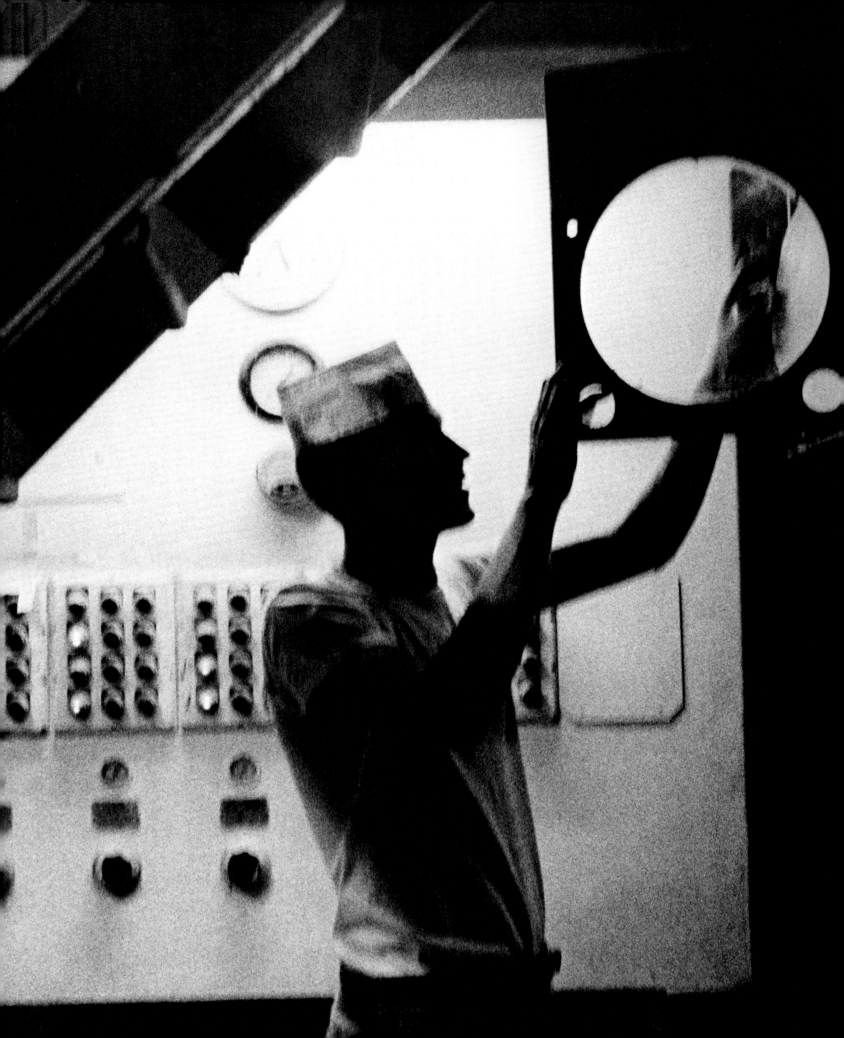

The factory job

With his deep love of the land, and anxious to secure the future for his growing family, Young Bill operated the Siskas' land on shares, lived in their house, and worked with his father. Ten years before, two families could have lived off the 335-acre farm his father owned; in 1965 it was not possible. As always, land had to be acquired; the home place was made up of what had once been three separate farms. Nations had carved political patterns on the land for their reasons; the early settlers had shaped it for their reasons; and now Bill, an echo of their spirit and John Rudolph Hammer's, had his. He was a settler, too. They had needed faith, an ax, a gun, and land; he needed faith and cash if he were to have the machines and land he required to remain a farmer. Even with Dorothy's paycheck there was not enough cash, and Young Bill netted only $2,000 a year, not enough to sustain him on the land. So he took a job in a feed factory eighteen miles away, working there nights after toiling all day on the farm.

Today it takes over a $100,000 investment to run a good Midwestern farm. Bill, Jr., was on his way. He worked hard, got some cash, and got the credit. He and Dorothy were able to pay for a tractor, jeep, manure spreader, plow, and a two-wheel trailer, none of them new, but they were theirs and did a good job.

In March of 1965, Bill, Jr., still had three years of factory work ahead of him. He, his dad, and Jim pause for a moment in the doorway of the Siska house. There Old Bill carries Judy in his arms. A loving grandpa, he checks in to play with the children. Jim already recognizes that he is a part of the family trio. With Bill he looks out of an empty farmhouse window at property that a young neighbor could not sustain. Bill would like to own it. Jim bangs away at a piano. At the factory, Bill works the late shift in order to remain a farmer.

MILDRED   Lots of people work two jobs, but I thought he was paying too high a price to be a farmer, and it was a worry to me. We weren't ready to retire, and he was so anxious to get to farming. I guess I had the feeling to tell him to just wait and have patience, just work your factory job, and wait till the time comes to take over the home place. But then, like he will say, "All things work out." They do believe that God takes one thing, but He sends another. When Junior was renting the Siska farm, the house was supposed to go with it. But the Siskas needed their house back. He and Dorothy had a dilemma. Where would he go? What would he do? They could still rent the land, but the owners wanted the house back.

I knew that he had to have a regular salary and I knew that he had to work at the factory. I wouldn't have thought much of him if he didn't get work. After all, he had a family to provide for. He could have worked at the factory and made his payments on a small place. But he wanted to get bigger and get out of the factory and do full-time farming. He wanted to have money for equipment and cattle and have enough equity to fulfill his ambitions, right now.

DOROTHY   I was working and the kids, a lot of the time, were at Bill's folks'. We were very much involved with each other. We lived at the Siskas' and Bill's dad did the milking for him. Bill was working at the factory all night and that was hard. But realize what his dad had to do. His dad had to milk his own cows and then come down there and milk ours. We couldn't have done it without his dad. But we couldn't have managed without the factory job. We weren't making ends meet. Bill thought about going back to work in the mine because he thought an extra job was the answer to stay on the farm. He almost felt like forgetting the farm and going and doing something else. But we had bought cows of our own and that was a start. Once you make a commitment like that, I think you're pretty well determined. With Bill, once he does something it's pretty hard to make him go back. I mean, if he sees something and he thinks it's the right way, he has to find out for himself if it is. So, he took the job in the factory. It was something to help the farm and be able to stay on it.

The job was bad for him—I mean, physically hard on him. He got so thin. He weighed 145 and he went with so little sleep. He would come home with all intentions of getting a lot of sleep, and then something would go wrong, or something needed doing. That was when he was working from 4 P.M. till midnight. Then he switched to another shift where he was working from midnight till 7:00. That's when he really went without sleep. It was sometimes thirty-six hours, easily, that I saw him go without sleep and he'd just kind of ... he wasn't really hearing you anymore. He was very tired. He worked that factory job starting in '65 and finished that one right after Jayne was born, late in '67. He was off for a while, but it didn't work out, so then he went back to work in the tire factory—that was in Freeport, about forty miles away.

BILL, JR.   I was farming on shares with the Siskas, and there wasn't enough money to support the family on. Then we went off shares and went the cash route. I rented. We only had thirty cows, and by the time you'd divide that in half, there was nothing left to live on. I did go on shares with Dad; he had a bigger operation. The reason I got the job was because I wanted to be a farmer and I had a disease problem with my pigs. I lost them all to TGE. I knew I wasn't going to make it without getting another job. So I got the job and straightened out.

I had my best years for income when I was working two jobs. But when you've got two incomes you're working for, you've got to give up something else. So I gave up sleep. I couldn't do it now, I'm too old for it. But at that time I was young and wiry, so that's what I did. The majority of the young farmers do that. That's about the only way you can get started, unless you're an heir or something like that, because when you go to borrow money, you've got to have some security to

put up. At first you have nothing, you don't have collateral. Dad had to sign for me, but I'd still have to make it, or they would take what he had. Once you get some collateral behind you, you can take it a little slower. When Dad signed for me, it meant the difference of me farming or not. At the bank they ask what you've got for collateral. I had a wife and car. I could have helped at Dad's place, but there wasn't enough money unless we could have gotten money to expand. The farm couldn't support us both. My idea was expansion, to get enough under my belt to do what we're doing now.

Hard years? They were hard-working years, and that's all right. If I was doing one or the other job, I would have no complaints. My farm was doing well and I had a good job at the factory, but I don't think I could have lived off that alone either. I made it, but I had to give it to my creditors, because that was the only way I could get collateral. When you buy seed, you can pay cash for it, or most of the time you can pay in thirty days. You can get longer credit, but you pay an awful price for it. You try to buy whatever you can in cash. If you can't, then you go see your banker and ask for a short-term loan. That's the main thing with farming: because your money only comes in at certain times, you've got to have credit.

Dorothy, Bill, and family– October, 1965

The land was turning to its autumn colors. There was field work to be finished. Young Bill looked for a farm of his own, rather than return to the trailer or to the home place. He was working the two jobs and, with his father's signature, could get credit. The Hammers have always had a good name. Jim was learning about that from the men by being with them whenever he could; alone, he would play in the yard or in the old shed, finding things to do among the discarded implements from which repair parts might be taken. Bill, Dorothy, Jim, and Judy posed for a family picture in front of the Siska house. At the home place, in another snapshot, a last one all together, they posed with the grandparents. Five years later, Celia Hickman, Dorothy's mother, was stricken suddenly and laid to rest.

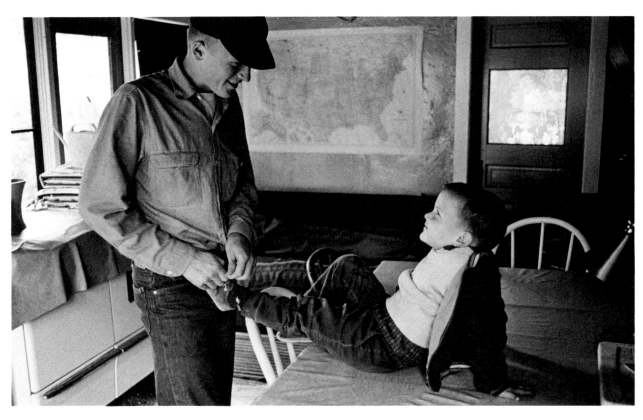

MILDRED   As long as we're all together, that's what matters. There's lots of things that rock the boat, but as long as we all stay in the boat, that's all that matters. I know what makes a family closer or puts you apart. You've got to have dependence on each other. Too much independence, and you don't need each other anymore. We depend on each other, we need each other. That makes a close relationship. If one of us would say, "Well, I could make it on my own," that's probably true, but we'd better add that we couldn't make it as well or enjoy it as much. I think that works in a marriage, too. I think a marriage can be ruined if one says, "I don't need you, I can get along without you just fine." Pretty quick you come to believe that, and you've got the other one convinced of it too, and so what have you got? Then you have nothing.

Like with Butch: he helps us and we help him in lots of ways you can't see. When he had to go look for a house, Bill was ready to sign for him. That was one way. But maybe a little of the faith he has in things he learned around here is another way. Like, he had to find a place, and someone came along and offered to sell him his place and gave him good terms—to pay it like rent. And then another neighbor found out he was sick and wanted to sell and said that Butch should have first chance at the place. That's like Butch says, "For every bad thing that happens, God provides something else. He takes care of it. If it wouldn't have been that I had to get out of the house, I wouldn't be where I am today." And maybe he wouldn't. Anyway, it's always been that we needed each other.

BILL, JR.   This house and property were for sale. The old guy had died and the relatives were trying to settle the estate. Some interests in Chicago were bidding on it. They wanted to pay a higher price than what I could afford. But I bid on it anyway, what I could afford and what I thought it was worth. I thought that place was sold a couple of times. Just when they went to sign, something would happen and the deals

would fall through. Then the owners came back to me and said I should have it at the price I offered. That was kind of a surprise to me. I mean, it seemed like that old man, up there, was watching, wanted me to have the land, and was pushing it my way. I figured if I got it or didn't get it, that's the way the Lord wants it, and that's the way it'd be. I just go along, figuring He'll take care of it.

I mean, I like the land and farming, and say I wanted to buy a farm. If it meant hardship on my family, or if I had to give it up, my family comes first. It would be financial reasons, and I would have to get another kind of a job. It wouldn't be because I didn't like the land, love it. It would be because I couldn't make a living on it. If it would come to my family, I would give up everything for them. Being together, doing the same things, is what's important. It's like the

238

whole family going out and feeding calves together—just doing stuff together that I could go out and do myself. It's liking the same things. I've done jobs that I didn't like and that's real fine. That's what my job is, to support my family, keeping them together. If I couldn't stay on the land, I'd just figure that's the way it's supposed to be, the way He wanted it. It'd work out. You can't always be happy.

DOROTHY I know what kind of farmer Bill is. Those Hammers, they're real farmers. I can't see him ever giving it up. Except maybe for his family. I think a successful family is one where the people like each other, just a lot of people that all get along together, live together, work together, and like each other. My family likes each other.

In 1966 Bill and Dorothy bought a small farm in the town—no more than a wide place in the road—where the elder Hammers were married. In a letter dated "Schapville, U.S.A., February 17" she wrote:

"We are finally settled on our little farm and we just love it. We moved in on Saturday, the fifth. The kids think it's swell, too. They have been investigating everything. Judy has fallen down two different sets of stairs and now has a beautiful black eye. Lucky thing she didn't hurt herself worse. Jim was four years old last Sunday, and the family all got together here. Grandma and Grandpa gave him some road-building equipment, and he was real thrilled. Monday, a little friend of his that lives across the field came over, and they had a big time playing with all these new toys. Bill is working the late night shift now, so he has been doing his sleeping in the daytime, and needless to say the kids make it rather tough for him. One good thing is that our basement is really neat and they do play quite a bit down there, so it cuts down the noise. Everyone is fine and quite busy. I'm still working a couple of days a week, sometimes three. . . ."

In another letter, on June 17, 1966, Dorothy wrote:

"Things seem to be going along pretty good for the entire Hammer family. Thank God. The kids love it here and they are growing like crazy. Bill and his dad have the corn all in and are getting ready for the haying season. They are making plans for a new milking parlor, milk house with a large bulk tank and all, and a giant pole shed or loafing shed for the cows. Since we have combined the herds, the milk checks are getting bigger and bigger. They are having problems getting a carpenter. They are all so busy around this area. It seems like everyone is building new barns and milking parlors. When they get it done, it will really be a sight to see. I'm really tickled, because both Bill and his dad work so hard and have for so long that they deserve to have things more modern. Right now we are looking for a dog for the kids. They just love them and play with the shepherd pups up at Grandma's all the time. Millie has a new white shepherd pup. We want a small dog for our house since we don't have a lot of room here. I have a real nice garden here and a big red raspberry patch that I hope will ready soon. We believe the move here was a good one for us and we are very optimistic about the future."

Schapville, U.S.A.

The harvest is in, and it is November, 1966. Bill and Dorothy can see the beginnings of accomplishment coming out of the dreams they have dreamed and the work they have done. In these late fall days, even with factory work and farm chores, Bill has time for Jim. At the Schapville place they have their own

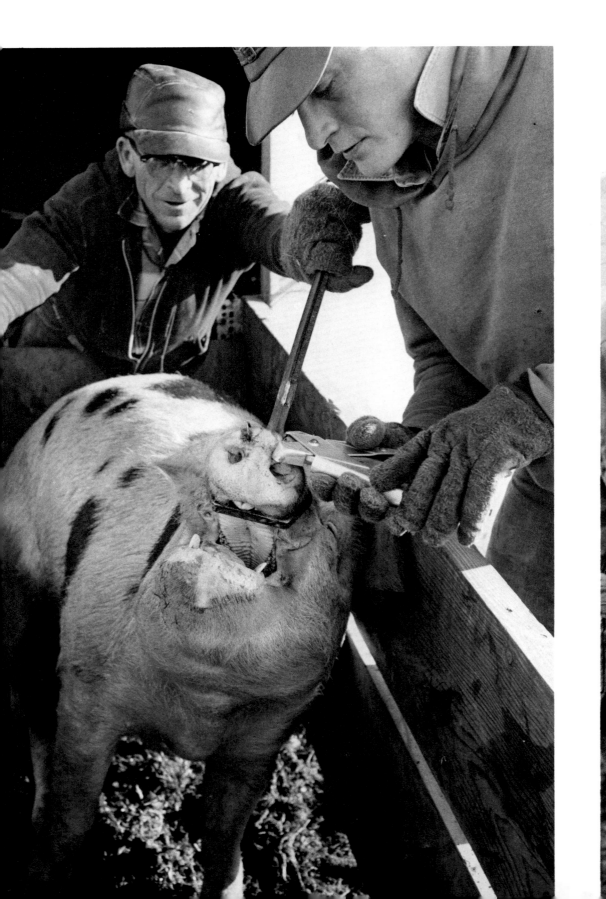

land on which to hunt, grow crops, and raise pigs. Jim watches Old Bill and his father "ring pigs" and stays out of their way. He has heard stories about little children being eaten by an old sow. Once, after his father was attacked by one, he heard him say,

"Normally they won't bother you, but when they've got little ones, they're protective. It's instinct. I went in there without a club or a board to protect myself and I took a chance which I probably shouldn't have. I have boards that I take in there that help protect your legs, not that they keep them from getting you, but it's part of the job."

They got the dog they wanted; she was bred and had puppies. When Bill handed them their first pups, Jim and Judy held them tenderly. It reminded Bill of his own childhood, not yet removed from the wonders of life and birth. In a playtime moment he scoops his children under his arms. Then it is early evening. Dorothy meets Bill at the front door of their house. He has to wash up

and leave for the factory. They pause for a moment in the fading light of a crisp night. The pet dog begs to come into the house, but farm dogs don't do that, and she must always stay outside, or now in the shed with her pups.

Bill and Dorothy have been in their place for ten months. It was not bought out of expediency or lack of choice. Dorothy says:

"We wouldn't have bought it if we didn't like it and the pride we could have in it. I always liked this place because I'd go with my dad on the mail route and see it."

Aside from farming, Ken Hickman worked for the post office.

"Whenever we'd come up that long hill, I thought that this was the cutest, nicest little place. When we first got this, I thought about how I always liked it. Then I was just liking the buildings and the look of the place. Now I like it because we've lived here and it's been good to us."

In reference to it and to their world, Dorothy calls it "Schapville, U.S.A."

Jim, amused by the various pronunciations and showing that he knows there are other places, says:

"Some people call it Shapeville, and some people call it Shop-ville, and some people call it Shapsville....I call it Schap-ville....Schapville, Tennessee."

A time for thanks

By March, 1967, the new milking parlor was complete. The loafing shed obscured the old barn door where Billy had paused on the night of his parents' anniversary eight years before. The father-son partnership flourished. Dorothy was pregnant with her third child. When they sat down to supper at Young Bill's house and said grace, it seemed like a special time for thanks. On Sundays or when the whole family is together, they always say grace. "Thank you for the food which we are about to receive and the blessings which you have bestowed upon us through Jesus Christ our Lord, Amen."

DOROTHY   You're always saying thanks to God, but not always in words. It's more a feeling of thankfulness. Like supper : the day is over, the work is done for the day, and you have a feeling of thanks for the food you have, for the day, and for having children. You're thankful for God's favors.

BILL, JR.   You don't ask Him for favors.

DOROTHY   You don't ask Him to make it rain for my crops so I won't lose mine.

BILL, JR.   You just take it for granted that He's going to supply you with enough to keep operating; you don't expect Him to make you rich. You don't call on God just for yourself.

MILDRED I said this to somebody not long ago: "I don't go to God asking Him for stuff as much as thanking him for what I got." I might ask Him not to take away what I got. I'm pretty satisfied with what I got. I read something in a book yesterday—Walt Whitman's—that struck me. I thought it expressed quite a thought. I'll read it to you. This is really like speaking from the grave, I mean, it's really kind of morbid in a way and it says:

> It is dark here underground—it is not evil or
>   pain here—it is blank here, for reasons.
> It seems to me that everything in the light and
>   air ought to be happy,
> Whoever is not in his coffin and the dark grave,
>   let him know he has enough.

There are a lot of people there, in the grave, if they had a choice—but they didn't have a choice—would take what I have, gladly.

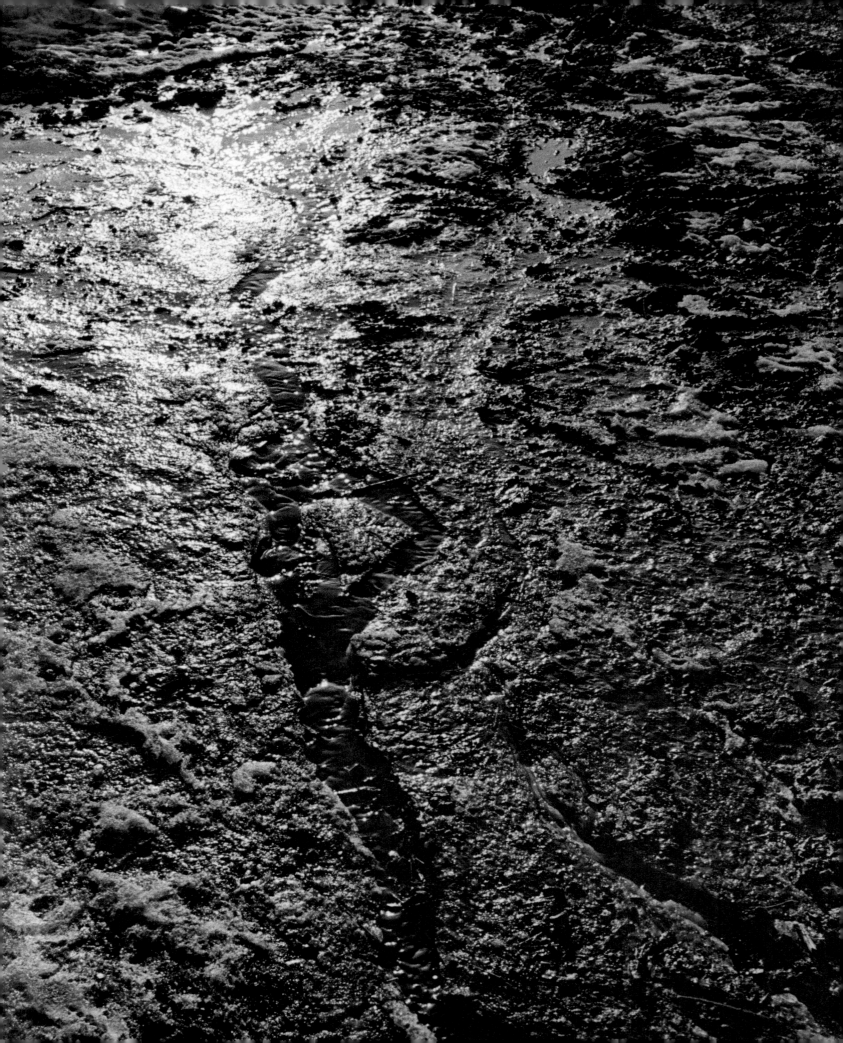

DOROTHY   Even if you think that everything'll turn out right, don't get the idea
           that you wouldn't ask God . . . .

           Young Bill broke the somberness and finished the sentence: ". . . for a little
           assistance, but I always figure to save my asking, there might be
           some time when I need Him more."

           Old Bill, Dorothy, Young Bill, and Mildred laughed.

MILDRED   "There's that story about the farmer that rejuvenated this plot of
           ground that hadn't been worth anything, and he had a beautiful crop
           on it. The minister came along and told him he had so much there to
           thank God for, and he said to the minister, 'Yeh, but you ought to've
           seen it when it was just God's alone.'" *They all laughed again. Young Bill
           added to that,* "We all work together with Him." *Old Bill reflected,*
           "Naturally, there's always a mystery to how things happen when
           you're farming, how things get growing from seeds. You don't
           understand it all, but you take it for granted and you're thankful that
           they happen as they do. We live with it. It all goes back to that. We
           live with it. We're thankful, but we don't think about it." *Then Mildred
           said,* "It gets to be like breathing."

Dorothy

Dorothy was born in Dubuque, Iowa. Her mother was from Benton, Wisconsin, her father from Scales Mound, where they were living in town at the time of her birth. Her paternal ancestors came from Germany at about the same time as the Hammers. Her grandfather farmed, sold insurance, and ran a restaurant in town. Later her father rented the farm from his father and does so to this day. Unlike Bill, she did not go to a country school but to town school. Then, as now, Scales Mound had a population of 400. Dorothy thinks that being a farm wife is the same as being a mother and wife anywhere. It does not depend on where one lives. Yet she has additional chores. She does field work. Once, working with Old Bill, she disked and he planted. At a break in the work a neighbor admired the working relationship. Old Bill told him, "Now you know why I am so proud of Dorothy."

DOROTHY   When they need me to do something, I have to be willing to do it. Besides, I enjoy being out on a tractor, and around here I don't see Bill that often during the day unless I'm working with him. Sometimes it's nine o'clock at night before I get to see him. I like being a farm wife—I mean, I like being away from people, being by myself with Bill and the kids.

Now look at it this way. Bill's folks live the way I like to live. At the home place you can look out and you can see your neighbors, but they're far enough away that you're not breathing down each other's throat. You can look out and say, "Oh, there's Carl out there today, making hay." That's a comfort and it's nice to be able to do. But you're looking at them far enough away.

In the city, if you don't get your lawn mowed, your neighbors might criticize you. If we don't get ours mowed, it doesn't show. I'm

262

busy enough, and then the days I can do it there might be rain. I mean, you want friends, you want people you can live with. But you don't want them breathing down your neck, and just because they do something, you have to do it. You ought to be able to do what you want in your own home and on your own place. Why should what your neighbors do dictate the way you have to do it? You have to do what's important. When it's time to make hay and people around you are making hay, all things being equal, then it's the time to make hay. So in that sense you have to do things when other people are doing them. But that's just because it's the right time. I don't like the feeling that I have to do something or have to be a certain way because somebody else is. That's just the way we feel about it. We don't like having people right on top of us. I don't think we'd ever buy land and sell lots off to people so that they could look down here at us like we're freaks in a sideshow. That's for the city and that's for people who are buying land to do that. They aren't farm people. If you want neighbors on top of you, you live in town.

I read quite a bit. When I read *The Godfather* it frightened me and yet it intrigued me, because our world is so far from that. We don't see the Mafia at work out here. It's hard to believe that that sort of thing goes on, and yet you know it goes on. Here, I really feel safe. I would hate to move from it. You can adapt to almost anything, but I feel safer in this area. It's part of my contentment. Sure, people get killed, but you don't hear all the time about murder; and most of the time we go away and leave the house open. We don't figure people are going to come and take anything. In a city I know you don't do that.

When I was growing up, I came from a different kind of farm life from what Bill had. I was more in town. We lived close to town. I could go to town in ten or fifteen minutes. I walked or rode my bicycle. It was a mile from my house. When I went cross-country, I cut through fields and it was less than that. I had lots of girlfriends in town, and my grandparents lived in town. I could stay with them. My life on a farm wasn't just all farm. Bill couldn't go that far—to get to town. He just had his farm. He was there all day. He had things to do there and he was a boy, he worked more around the farm. Maybe that's why farm men feel closer to their past and things than women do, unless you were the tomboy type that did all the chores and did all the things that the boys would normally do, you might have that feeling. If you were out with the sick cows, and so on, and saw them nursed back to health, and all that kind of thing, you would have more of a feeling for that. I didn't do many things on the farm. As soon as I was able to drive the tractor we would unload hay, but I never had to milk. I fed calves. I thought of myself as a farm girl, but I wasn't the tomboy-type girl. I mean I was more in Girl Scouts, music lessons, and I was in town a lot.

I used to do some of the chores with my father, but I remember thinking of it as just something I had to do. I don't remember that I liked it all that well. He's always been the sub mail carrier, never the main one, just did when the other guy didn't. So he'd haul for two weeks for sure every year, sometimes more. We always used to go with him—it was allowed then, now it isn't. That was a big thing, to get to go and do that. I always liked going with him on the mail route. I helped my mother. I was always around for that, because girls naturally are, to help clean and cook, bake.

I have an older sister, three years older than me, and a brother, seven years younger than me. I'm the middle child. We fought a lot. Of course that was really the difference between living near town and living the way Bill did. I had my own friends that I played with. My sister is different than I. She's more quiet, she could amuse herself. My brother was a brat, as far as I was concerned. We didn't have to depend on each other. I could go to town. We didn't move to the farm until I was five or six, and I used to fight with the neighbor kids.

I wanted to be a mother and wanted to have my own kids. I had my own pictures of what I wanted them to be. It isn't that way and I'm not disappointed. They're all three good kids. Good-hearted. All three are different. Judy is sensitive. She feels things very much, very deep. Jayne is the type that you could tell her, "Don't touch that iron, it's hot, it'll burn you," and she'll walk right over and touch it. She has to find out for herself, and then she will probably cry because she burned herself. If you tell Judy the same thing, she'll listen. She tries her darnedest to please. We don't always appreciate it. She's very little bother and needs the least attention. I really feel that out of the three of them, when Judy looks back on her childhood, she'll probably feel that she wasn't treated right, that there was something missing. You know, I can recognize this, but I really don't know what to do about it. That makes me feel bad. As a mother I should know automatically, and I don't.

I was a second child like Judy. I felt my sister did everything first and my brother, as a boy, was different from us. I was like Jayne. I tried to get attention, although I remember too that I used to bend over backwards to please my parents because I thought I had to. I was good in school, but I *tried* to be good in school. It seems that you do everything for the oldest, for the first one. I guess that's natural. Like, Jim got the first bike and he got the mini-bike. He was ready for it sooner. I never got anything first. I got the leftovers. Hand-me-downs. That's why I think it's important that Judy got her bike. She was driving around on a second-hand thing that had no tires. You got to play it fair with your kids. But you've got to watch it, because you can carry that too far. They'll catch on and play on that. Kids are no dummies.

Jim is real smart. And Bill and Jim are quite a bit alike. They both like—love—the farm. I think Bill likes work better than Jim. Jim is more inclined to find an easier way or the shortest way to arrive at the same thing. Maybe that's this generation. Where Bill

had to find things to amuse him—Jim does that, too—he's got more things. Our children don't have to make things, find things for themselves to do all the time. I remember we used to walk out in the fields at home and we did a lot of things like play in the haymow, build forts. You always had something to do. You never said, "Well, what can I do today?" Our kids have had television and have grown up with television. They don't have to go out and work for their own entertainment as much as we had to.

I look forward to my children grown up. Seeing how they turned out, I guess. I hope that Jim turns out all right. I think he will. I hope that he doesn't get into a lot of trouble as a teenager. There's all sorts of trouble and there's getting more all the time. It seems like the kids around here have newer and faster cars, for teenagers, than what they do in the big cities. More than likely Jim will have a car of his own, and I hope he isn't crazy with it. I hope that he doesn't get with a crowd that steals and ransacks houses. That's getting to be a big thing around here, too. I really don't know how to keep him from doing it. How did my folks do it with me? They never sat down with me and said, "Dorothy, you don't do this and you don't do that," but I knew there were things that weren't right and that I shouldn't do. Jim listens to me, maybe with one ear. He listens to his father more than me. Yes. He's with his dad more. Jim and I don't see eye to eye on very many things. Being a woman might enter into it.

Jim right now wants to be a farmer. If he wanted to be on the farm, we'd try to see that he was and help him if we could. Our situation is such that he could easily follow into it. I mean, there is a place for him if he really wants it. Yes, I'd like to see that, and we're working to build up the place. But I have two girls to consider, too. You can't do it all just thinking of Jim.

Yes, I look forward to my children grown up. I think it'll be interesting to see them picking boy friends and girl friends. We kind of wonder what they're going to look for. And Jim, whether he decides to be a farmer ... well, it's like you're writing chapters and waiting to see how it ends ... it's a story. It'll be a good story, I think, if you teach your children how to live with people and yet to have a certain sense of being your own man, doing your own, living the way you want to. You can do this no matter what you do or where you live. You don't have to grow up on a farm and have farm life be the only way you know. But if you teach your children the right way, they can make a transition into another life, live in the city, and still have the things they learned when they were on the farm. I think that if you can get along with people, you can get along with them anywhere. And you have to learn that when you're young.

I think that I'd like to see Bill have more. Like the tractor, the new tractor. I went with him and looked at it. I was thrilled for him, because it was what he wanted for a long time. I never saw him that excited. We talk about major things we buy, like the tractor, or big things I want—new linoleum, kitchen carpeting. He says, "Go ahead and get what you want, but I want to see the color." But I just go ahead and get it. He knows what he wants in a truck or tractor, and I know what I want in carpeting. The house is my part of the partnership, but I wouldn't think of doing any big thing without asking him. I can buy pretty much what I want. There are always things you can get. Like I say, I think I'd like to see Bill have more—machinery, things that he needs. And then I think we'd like having a real nice place. I mean, we've got a nice place, but it could be a lot nicer ... the buildings all painted ... not that we have to have all new, because you can make an old place look nice if you try. It's like this area. It's old and you know most everybody. It's a nice feeling. Especially if you come from a good family and they haven't a lot of skeletons in the closet. People say, "Well, you're a Hickman," or "You're a Hammer. I know your dad and grandpa." Having roots is a good thing.

The inheritance–August, 1970

Young Bill had quit the factory job and smoking, and had gained both weight and time to work on his farm. Half his life ago, at fourteen, his picture had been made while his mother painted a mark at his height on a barn door; now, at twenty-nine, he posed for another. At eighteen he had his name painted on the pickup truck door. It said: "WILLIS A. HAMMER & SON." At half the age his father had been, Jim, at nine, had his name painted on. It now said: Willis Sr.—Willis Jr.—Jim HAMMER." Old Bill commented, "Well, things just happen faster these modern days."

MILDRED   Grandpa Hickman printed that on there. He's quite a painter, you know. I don't know if Bill and Junior knew he was going to do it, but he knew they wouldn't care. Anything concerning Jim, they wouldn't care.

DOROTHY   Bill said that it's funny to see Jim do things for the first time, things that he did. You think "Gee! The first time he's driven the tractor, the first time he's disked." Bill gets to see all these things. This means a lot to him. I think any father would miss seeing that; you know, boy!, when I did that for the first time, that was really a great feeling and then be able to see your son do it, too. That's a new great feeling for any father.

What would I say is the greatest heritage a mother and father can give? I think that has an awful lot to do with the way you grow up. So far our kids have lived with a mother and father, family, who love each other. I think they know this. They don't live in a constant turmoil, parents fighting. I think they live in a home that's happy, where you do your share. This is why we think that feeding the calves is important. It gives the children a sense of all of us having to do something and being able to get along. We don't, all the time. This morning was great. They were quiet. But usually we are all fighting. I try to tell them that if they listened and followed the way I told them to feed, things would go smooth. But Jim has his ideas. He'll try it, and if it doesn't work out, he gets mad. Then the girls get mad because he's mad at them. It just turns into a turmoil; but I think you learn from that. Because eventually they will be able to go out there and feed, and it will be one small way where they've learned to do something and where they are actually helping. It's one of the first chores we've had down here. Jim helps in the hog barn; he gets the feed. But the girls don't and have never really had any chores and this is a way of getting them involved. When they get older, those

girls will be helping making hay, and doing things like that, because I think they'll want to.

Jim's a lot of help this year. He was a lot of help last year, but he's bigger and stronger and this year he can do more. He disked for the first time this year with the tractor.

Young Bill would like to pass this on to his children: "To find something they like, besides liking it for the money. Like the farm. More occupations pay a lot more money than farming, but that's what I like."

OVERLEAF: *The cows, their longing bellows satisfied, have come to the barn. In the shadowless gray of evening, the pause between darkness and the dim light of a waning day, no creature calls, no machines are heard. All is silence. Even the wind is still, waiting to capture the moment of the earth's sweet breathless sigh between sunset and moonrise.*

Summer language

During summer vacation Jim corrected Judy's grammar. "Judy! You can't say 'has went!' In school I wouldn't say it; the teachers bug you all the time about it when you say 'has went' or something like that. Like we used to say, 'me-'n-John,' and the teacher would go, 'I didn't know John was mean'." Judy looked apprehensive at the horror of displeasing her new teacher next year as she now had her older brother. Jim felt bad then and with sweet, patient calm comforted her, "That's all right, Judy. Around here you can use summer language."

It was summer—July, 1971. It was the time to relax and be yourself, to grow, to be proud to work with the men, and to have fun. That is what Jim was thinking. Already he measured up to the height of his father's first mark on the barn door. Jim liked the Hammer ways, and his family took pride in him.

In the field where Bill, Jr., had once chased sheep, he now helped Judy and Jim bridle Jim's horse, Sparkle. Jim spent a great deal of time with Sparkle, and sometimes shared him with Judy. Bill had added some land to his original purchase in Schapville, and on it he put a new hog barn. Jim would help Bill load hay, which Bill then carried to the hog barn. In the early morning they would check the fences together.

JIM   I have a pet cow, Lillian, that's part Dad's and part mine, and I have two dogs, two cats—we have eight cats altogether, but I have two of them for my own—and I've got Sparkle, my horse. I think he pretty well knows me. He knows when I come along it's either riding or something. Old Domino? He died. I really liked that dog. His son looks pretty much like him. I've had four German shepherds already ... no! Two or three. Duke was the first one and he was run over. First time Mom ran over his leg with a car; it didn't hurt him. And then the second time the milk truck ran over his leg and crushed his leg in three places, and they didn't know if they could fix it, and it would take two hundred dollars for two operations and they still weren't sure they'd work, so Dad put him to sleep. Then we had another dog called Duke—we decided to call him Duke after the other dog.

I went fishing in our creek. I caught thirty-four chubs. I ate them—not me, I didn't eat all of them! We shared them with all the family. I ate one, it had too many bones. I only ate one and that's it. If you fry them good, Grandma says that you can eat it all, the bones will get so soft. It only took us an hour to catch them. All we had to do was throw our fishing lines in and pull them out. Maybe we can dig us some worms and go fishing tomorrow morning. It's right on our land.

Swimming is fun ... and riding my mini-bike.

JUDY   That's your fun, not ours.

JIM   Girls' fun is getting their brothers mad ...

JUDY   ... swimming, riding horses ...

JIM   ... being scared of worms ...

JUDY   ... fishing.

JIM   I've got something I've got to do, not looking forward to it. That's making hay.

JUDY   My friend and I are going to push the bales out ...

JIM   ... on my head!

JIM   My best friend is Steve; he is my *very* best friend. I don't have any other guy about my own age—he's m'best friend. Steve is six months older than I am, but we get along so good. It's hard to believe, but I used to go over there every day and spend the whole day. Come at nine in the morning and stay till six at night. If you go up in our corn field and look straight over, you'll see a brick house. That's where he used to live. He moved to Wisconsin. His dad used to be preacher.

One of the good things of growing up on the farm is not living in cities. From what you hear about them, they aren't the best things to live in. I can play basketball on my own court, and you've got no people, like in an apartment building, no people living together right

next door where you've got to be so quiet. We can yell and scream all we want. And we can build tree houses and have friends down to go swimming. We try to go a lot to Shullsburg. They've got a great big swimming pool. Sometime I'd like to get a creek or dam up a spring and make a pond and have Dad push some dirt in there. We don't do much swimming in the creeks.

I want to be a farmer, because I like the work. You don't have anybody over you all the time. You judge it by your own sense. You

290

don't have somebody telling you how to do it all the time. Like in other jobs, there's always somebody over your head. I'd like to be my own boss. Oh, doing my chores sometimes gets a little hard, getting the cows and stuff. Dad worked harder when he was a boy. I don't need to work as much, probably because there's a lot more machines. But yesterday I worked pretty hard baling, throwing those bales around ... ha-ha, throwing myself around. My favorite work is chopping—and, oh, it's just fun sitting there, going asleep in the green chop [freshly cut and chopped hay].

The chores I do, Dad gave them to me: scrape out the barn, get the barn ready, help make hay, get the cows by myself, help feed the calves, and this year the tractor (I got to throttle it and steer it and all) first time. Oh! And I've got to plow. I was proud of myself. I've always wanted to help in the field, but there was nothing for me to do except hook the harrow behind the disk and stuff. I like the work.

Chickens? That's not my job; that's Grandma's job most of the time. That's women's work; they're usually the ones that want them. They do the cooking and stuff like that, and Mom helps in the field, helps us all over, rakes hay when we need help.

I like being a boy. Get to do more stuff. Like my sisters, they can't go with my dad as much as I can. We're alike. We both like living on the farm. We both like to do a lot of things, the same things. He likes to play basketball and I like to do that. He likes building and I like building. Learned a lot from him. I like to help him; just, oh, I guess I figure I might as well hang around as much as I can. He won't be here all the time. So I might as well. I'll try farming with him—when I grow up.

Do you know what I think when you say "the land"? I think I call it "the ground." In a kind of a way I love the ground. Because you've got to have the ground to live. It grows all things, you eat the plants, you've got to have ground to survive. Do you know what I like about the farm? Well, one thing is that you've got a lot of space to do what you want.

I consider two places my home place. One at our place and one at Grandma's place. I suppose I'll be living either at the place where we live now or at my Grandma's. I'd want to live close to Mom and Dad. I'd get married, I hope so. What kind of a girl? One that won't mind working. We'd have a son first . . . and name him James Alan Hammer, Jr., because I would like him named after me because that's the way Grandpa did to Dad. Then we could all be together. That's a family. Some people to be with. People you like.

What did Mom teach me? For one thing, she taught me how to mow the lawn. She showed me how to tie my shoes. That's one of the things I'll never forget. I used to sit there all morning tying my shoes. And she tries to teach me to live decent. Like some people don't have a very good life because they don't settle down in one place. They move a lot. Like they move to one place and don't stay very long. They could live in Illinois for a while and then move to California. I like Illinois; it's just my home state. She'd like me not to growl, be a grump. Like with the land: sometimes I feel pretty awful about it when something goes wrong, when the crops won't grow right—there's too much clay; when those animals were dying. It was awful, felt awful.

I like all the cows we have. Can't say the same for the pigs. It depends. If they chase me out, I don't like them too well. Yesterday morning one of them got at me. I jumped over the fence though. That old sow! I had to kick her in the nose, and then she turned around and went away. Those sows, sometimes they'll eat their own babies. They'll smother them, too.

Let's see. Then Mom wants me to be a good Christian—to go to church every Sunday—at least every Sunday that you can. Pray at night. Worship God. Send money to the poor. Love your enemies. Be thankful, like for the farm, and if the crops go well. Well, even if they don't. And I'm thankful for my mom and my dad and my grandma and my grandpas, my cousins, and my sisters, and all my friends.

JAYNE

The crops needed rain. On the Fourth of July it came. Bill and his family drove to Shullsburg to watch the parade. Dorothy said: "I couldn't tell you all about being an American except in a parade like on the Fourth, when you hear that music. I like the band and seeing the flag go by. You just feel good. I feel it in myself. I know that I'm an American, and I wouldn't be anything else, because I think this country's a good country. I never had to go out and fight for it, and it's got a lot of troubles. Bigger troubles than I could ever handle. Still, you feel good living in it. I feel good living in this state. I can't imagine living anywhere else. It would seem funny not to write 'Scales Mound, Illinois.' When I was a cheerleader, I used to yell 'S-C-A-L-E-S M-O-U-N-D, yea! Scales Mound!' Wouldn't want to do that anywhere else."

Back at the home place, after the parade, a beef roast cooked over an outdoor fire. Barney and his family, friends from downstate Illinois, had brought the beef with them and cooked it. After dinner the children played in the yard. Barney's son-in-law and granddaughter stretched out in the hammock to the happy sounds in the yard and the contentment of the home place.

Then the holiday was over and it was chore time. Old Bill and Young Bill paused a moment to reflect on the joy of the day. Then the cows were driven to the milking parlor.

The next day, Bill spoke of his relationship to Jim: "I very seldom take him fishing or horseback riding. Actually, all it is out here is work. And if you don't enjoy your work, then you're in bad shape. I think Jim enjoys it, and I'm happy about that." In the empty hay barn, soon to be filled to the rafters, father and son paused for a moment to talk. "When I grow up," said Jim, "I'm going to be like Dad."

Birthdays

A decade had passed since Jim was born and brought home from the hospital over blacktops that had been snow-scraped through the white-covered hills and valleys of Wisconsin and Jo Daviess County, Illinois. Over these paths that had first been Indian and trapper trails, then the mud roads of the lead haulers, of stage lines, of farmers, and were now lovely respites from superhighways James Alan Hammer had come home to the land that had fostered his father, his father's father, and three generations before that, and their women, too.

Now it was Sunday, February 13, 1972, and Jim became ten; the land looked just as white as it had ten years before. The family gathered at the home place to celebrate Jim's birthday and Janet's, for she was born on that day too. They shared a cake that Mildred had baked and decorated as she had learned to at cake-decorating lessons in a church-sponsored class.

Janet now had four children: Brenda (aged sixteen), Bonny (fourteen), Bryan (eight), and Betty (five). Brickner had two jobs. The first one was at the John Deere factory in Dubuque. He drove over seventy-five miles each working day for thirteen years, and during that time he bought his farm, improved his buildings, and raised beef cattle. Now he was through at the factory. He and Janet had bought and begun to operate the grocery store in Scales Mound. They had modernized it, extended the hours, and expanded the variety of items. Now it is one of the finest stores in the area, and people come from miles around to shop. They still have the farm, too.

After the large birthday dinner and after the cake was cut, there were presents. Jim had already received his mini-bike from his parents and now got a wrist watch from Bill and Mildred so that he could "remember the time."

MILDRED   I guess when you celebrate any birthday, you're celebrating everything that ever happened good to you, and all of us being here.

Then Jim said: "Take a picture of me against the barn. See if I got any taller since the last time."

311

In April it was cold and too muddy to plow. Jim saw to his chores of finding the cattle and getting them to the barn. Bill tended to the evening milking in the modern milking parlor at the home place. But the growing season was coming, and with it a new cycle.

Cycles

From the crest of any hill one could see gravel back roads slashing through plowed fields to cross-road towns. There church spires, the tallest structures around, maintained comforting vigils over the people, the houses, and even the towering silos. It was a time to be born, to plant, build, laugh, dance, embrace—a time to keep, a time to love, and a time for peace. For Jim it was all these things and another season of growing, learning, working into the ways of his father and grandfather. When the cycle began again, it was May, 1972.

BILL, JR.   When he disked his first field this year, it was in the big job, the John Deere. I was in the tractor with him in case something would go wrong. With that one you don't have to shift, but he could if he had to. He worked it for himself for the first time. He made all the corners and turned it and he did it all by himself up there in the cab. It's sort of amazing to think that somebody you made is up there where he's getting to the age to do that. He did pretty good for his age, too.

There's not too many chores Jim has to do. Can't really let him around the pigs too much. You never know when there's a mean one. When I was growing up, we didn't have as many pigs. I'd go along when Dad went to look at them. I didn't like milking when I was young, and Jim doesn't like the pigs too much, but someday he'll come around to it too. When it comes haying time, he's there every day helping us make hay. He might not have to do much, but whatever he can do he does well. Around the machinery he knows his way pretty much, but he likes to think he knows more than he really does.

316

The cows were giving birth to overlarge calves, and they went "down" paralyzed. Jim's job was to find them. When he did, Bill moved the tractor into the area to hoist them to their feet. Bill said, "You've got to get them up and moving around if they're going to have a chance to make it." Commenting on the father-son relationship, Dorothy said: "Jim has a feeling that he's got to be a man. You can tell in the way he wants to listen and do things right, do what I tell him. Yet he doesn't

*want to think he's a momma's boy—I don't think he'll ever have to worry about
being that. I didn't know Bill at Jim's age, so I didn't see how he got along with his
dad. One way is the same. They're together. Jim goes with his dad every chance he
gets. He went since the time when he probably shouldn't have. Seems that he must
have always wanted to be with his dad."*

BILL, SR.   As a father you get more overcautious, and you have to watch it. The machinery today is much more treacherous than what we had. It's bigger, more complex, and you'd better know what you're doing. Years ago you could spread manure with a fork; it's pretty hard to do it the wrong way, or get hurt. But now, with a tractor, you can do three men's work with it. And you have to have them to keep up with the times. There's a law now that says you have to be over sixteen to drive a tractor—unless it's on your dad's farm. It makes it rough on these twelve- to fourteen-year-old kids today. They can't go out as summer help and earn themselves a little spending money. There's some, I imagine, that get hurt, but there are a few that get bumped off in the city and they aren't even near a tractor. Farm labor is too high-priced, and so you've got to put money into bigger equipment to do the job. Then you've got to have somebody run it, and it has to be you or, because of the law, your own son. It makes it practical to have sons—so they can help out with the tractor work.

Dorothy climbed onto the tractor and disked 140 acres in the warm, promising days of May. She and Bill had just celebrated their eleventh wedding anniversary, and in June she would help make hay, feed calves with the children, walk in the fields, cook and sew, and she would reach her thirtieth birthday.

By July the corn was over knee high. Bill and Jim walked along with Old Bill driving the tractor. When it was haying time, Young Bill used the big new John Deere. Jim would run after him, hoping that Bill would let him drive it again—or at least let him ride in it—so that they could be together. He used his mini-bike for scooting up and down the hills and valleys and for chasing the cows. Bill said: "I get a charge out of him riding the mini-bike, because I remember how much fun I had on the one I made for myself. His is a little better than what I had."

BILL, SR.   I started in plowing with horses when I was ten years old, and chores, and milking cows. I liked the responsibility; definitely, it gives you a sense of responsibility, plus family life and working together. Jim's tried hand-milking, but he doesn't get much. His hands are not too big. The Hammers are noted for their large hands. The Evanses are a more dainty type. Butch's hands are longer, and they're always getting in the way and getting something taken off.

BILL, JR.   Couple of the tips of the fingers, sewed back on. One was on the jeep, the other two I chopped them off in a chain . . .

MILDRED   . . . on a motor bike he built. He built one, but he forgot to cover the chain.

BILL, JR.   It tipped over, and I reached back to grab myself and got caught in the sprockets—got my fingers. But you've got to learn to work with machinery. Right now my plans are to have stuff so that if Jim wants to come in with me someday, I'll be in a position that he can. I hope he's smarter than me and that he does everything better than I did it. You can probably tell I'm proud of him by all the stuff he's got. If I had half the things he's got when I was a kid, I don't know what I would have done. That isn't the way to show your feelings, but most people do it that way. I mean, how many kids do you know that have got a horse, mini-bike, regular bike, and just about anything they want, as long as they're not getting into trouble?

I've got two girls, too. I have to watch out for them. They have shares in what I've got, too. What part is theirs depends on how much work Jim's done and how old he is when he takes over.

DOROTHY   We accept things the way they are. Like living on a farm, we accept that because that's just the way it is. We like being part of a family because we've always been part of a family. You accept what you've

336

got and who you are and try to work it out. I heard once that one door is never shut that another one isn't opened to you. This is always true. It seems like one phase of your life ends, but another whole new one is always waiting. I mean, I was just twenty-nine and now I'm thirty. They tell me things happen when you're thirty. I hated it all the year I was twenty-nine, thinking I was going to be thirty. My twenties were good years, a lot happening. I had three children and they're all about in school. We moved; we bought two farms. All this happened when I was in my twenties. I kind of hated to see that end. When you're a teenager you think, "I can't wait until I'm twenty-one." Well, what's there to look forward to now? You get old, but I think you're only as old as you let yourself be. Bill and I are getting these wild clothes, and he says, "I'm too old for that, don't you think?" I just don't feel that way. I figure if he dresses young and thinks young, he'll stay young. If you think you're old, your life's like you are—you'll get old. I know lots of people who get old and suddenly try to be young. Doesn't work. The trick is to stay young.

On a December day the family again posed for their pictures in the light of a second-floor window at the home place.

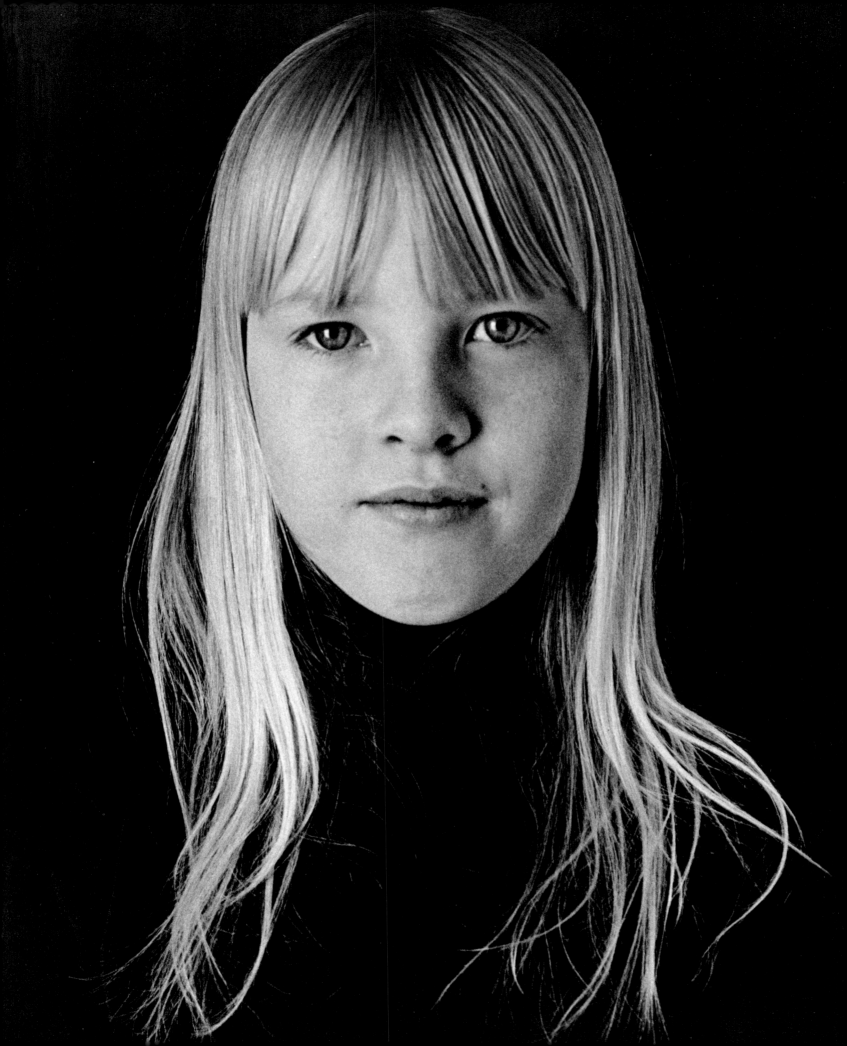

Epilogue

Powerful forces first led me to the Hammers and suggested that each fragmented act of their lives I witnessed was worth preserving. Strength, goodness, harmony, universal order, exist in their world. Betrayal does not. These are the qualities I have attempted to show in this album. It tells not so much how the world really is all the time as how it could be, perhaps how it should be—the way it is for the Hammers. Out of friendship alone, nothing more, they consented to become the allegory for those things. In authentic ways their lives say for me what I cannot say without them.

The Hammers are more to me than a metaphor of the spiritual and American heritage of a farm family. Yet, with them and with other fragments of experience, I have learned that what I was taught as a child is, or can be, mostly true. I learned that there has been only one true creative act: the making of something out of the nothingness of a void, an act performed only by God, the sole creator. All else is circumstance, experience, invention, innovation—discovery, more than anything else—and a putting together in a particular fashion of things that have always existed. I learned that life is about nothing, absolutely nothing at all; it becomes greater than it appears to be only when someone cares to give it special significance. This is what makes life a meaningful gift to mankind alone, the discoverers of the words "wisdom," "existence," "begin," and "end." I have learned that farming can be an art, and that this is true of any human endeavor. And I have come to believe in the mystical. The Hammers

might sum all this up as "the way things are meant to be." There are others in the world like the Hammers, but my lens focused on them, and perhaps that, too, "was meant to be."

I was talking of such things to Dorothy one morning after the calves had been fed and the breakfast dishes put away. Occasionally the screen door slammed at the Schapville house as Jim, Judy, or Jayne came to settle an argument or ask a question. Outside, the circular noise of a pump creaking away was heard, and so was the squeal of a pig. Inside, the windows framed diamonds of sunlight flashing off the green cornstalks.

Dorothy said, "I see it this way. There's God in every day. You wouldn't have a day unless there's a God. Because, well, you see it in the crops as they grow and start from nothing but seed and plowed ground. Then in a few months you go out and look and you've got corn. You also have weeds. I mean, we believe in God.

"I'm more of a churchgoer than Bill is. I always have gone every Sunday, and that's the way it is. Now I teach Sunday school. But we don't think it's all that necessary that you have to go to church, be right *in* church, all the time. Bill doesn't take that much of an active part in church, but I think Bill is religious. He believes in God; you can tell that by the way he farms. We know that God is always there, but we might not be talking about it all the time. Bill believes that if the Lord wants it, then it's going to be that way. He believes that about a lot of things. I'm trying to, but I don't always see how it works out that way. He always seems to think that if it is the right time for something, then it will be. I don't know if he's ever had that put to a real severe test—whether if he had a real catastrophe he'd still look at it as if that's the way it's going to be, then that's the way it's going to be. Or whether it would really crush him. He's terribly close to his dad. If something'd ever happen to his dad, or to his children, I don't know how he would come out of it. But Bill's very strong. He has a lot of belief and he's always found a way to meet any problem."

352

The cows had been milked, the light of the day had faded away, the chores were done. Bill, Jr., and I were sitting across from each other at the table in the kitchen of the home place. Dorothy was at home with the children and Bill, Sr., and Mildred had gone to visit friends. My youngest son was off riding Jim's mini-bike in the darkness after we had all cautioned him about the bats in the woods, the German shepherd guard dog, and the bull let loose with the herd on the hillside pasture. My son was a few years older than Bill was when I first met him. I was anxious about this night riding, and Bill calmed me. "Don't worry," he said. "He looks like he knows what he's doing. Those kids can do a lot more than what we think they can do, and they probably worry about staying out of trouble more than we can."

It was strange to think that this man in front of me was the boy I had seen grow to manhood, have children, and become a father giving a father's advice. He was right. Off in the distance, and coming closer all the time, I could hear the sound of the mini-bike returning to the yard, and then the motor being shut off at the barn. Now there was quiet.

After a few moments Bill said, "Seems like sometimes the Lord works against me, against what I think I want. Sometimes things work for me. But God is there just every day. I'm even more religious than lots of people think I am. I don't like a lot of the new ways. If something was good enough years ago to do it that way, why all of a sudden change? I like a lot of the old ways.

"Nowadays people do stuff that years ago they'd practically be banished from the territory for doing, and now they don't think anything of it. I think you have to be as honest as you can be. Just follow the rules as much as you can. There's so many of them that everybody breaks a few. What rules? I think the Ten Commandments are about as good as anything. I mean, they pretty well cover anything. Some people think that religion is more for the poor people than it is for the rich people. The poor people don't have anything

except belief in their faith. When you're rich, you forget about it and you might say, 'Boy! I'm self-sustaining, I don't need it.'

"When bad things happen, it might be that the Lord's testing you out. I mean, I've never had anything real bad, but I've had a lot of problems—livestock dying, and that—and I actually think that it prepares you for something ahead of you. Like when that relative died: his sons took it pretty well, because they were away from him and only saw him once in a while, and they were more or less what you'd call weaned. I don't know what it will be like, you know, if something happened to Dad. We work together; we're together a lot of the time. I know it's going to happen someday. If it happened in a natural way it would be bad, but not as bad as if it was an accident or something like that before his time. I really don't know what I'd do.

"I guess some have got to be born, others have got to die. It's the Lord's act. If everybody lived, this place would be awful crowded. There would be no way of existing. I'd say you've just got to have faith or you could go insane. Like I'm constantly afraid that something will happen to one of the kids. I mean that you've just got to have faith that He wants to let them live. If He takes them, you'll just have to cling to Him all the more. I don't know how well I'll believe that if it ever happens, but I'll have to cling to Him, because that's the way He wanted it."

There is serenity now in a place I know like no other. It's around Scales Mound in the deeply etched panorama of Jo Daviess County, in the northwest corner of Illinois, where the land is crayon green in the spring and fleece white in the winter, and stays that way until the thaw.

ACKNOWLEDGMENTS

I wish to thank the following people for their aid and encouragement through the years of this project: Phillip Drell, Vories Fisher, Jerry Hurley, Jack Star, Howard Chapnick, Robert and Alice Cromie, Tereska Torres Levin, Mirron Alexandroff, Captain Harold Cowell, Dr. Cornelius Vermeulen, Dr. Milton Robin, my editors, Paul Anbinder and Margaret L. Kaplan, the designer, Robin Fox, and my friends and neighbors in Schapville and Scales Mound who remained themselves while I worked with my cameras. Special thanks go to Meyer Levin for putting me in touch with Harry N. Abrams, and for reading the text and making many helpful suggestions.

That which hath been is that which shall be,
And that which hath been done is that which shall be done;
And there is nothing new under the sun.

ECCLESIASTES 1:9